THE RUGBY

WORLD CUP GUIDE 2003

BRENDAN GALLAGHER

CARLTON
BOOKS

Contents

6 Nov 1999: David Giffin of Australia holds aloft the Webb Ellis trophy after victory over France at the Millennium Stadium, Cardiff. Australia won 35–12.

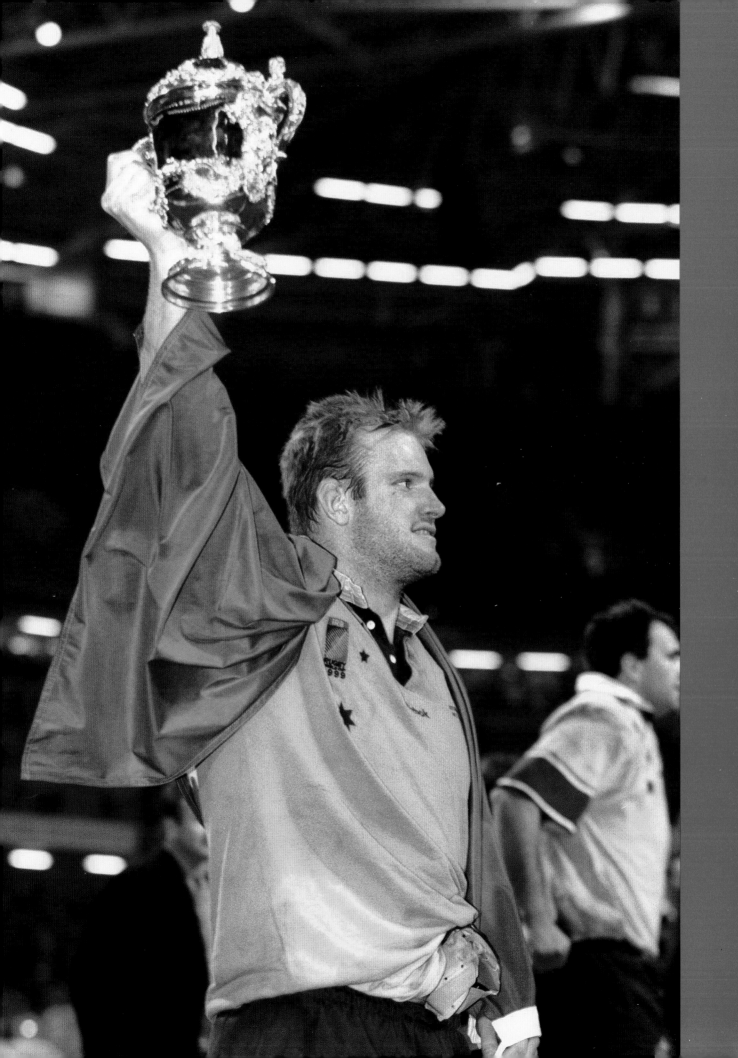

Welcome to the Party!

If there is one thing Australians know about, it's sport and how to stage major sporting events. The Rugby World Cup 2003 is going to be a major success – you can put your house on it.

The build-up and the politics may have been a little fraught – in particular when the International Rugby Board took away New Zealànd's co-host status – but our Australian hosts will make the tournament memorable in all respects.

The Aussies have an instinctive feel for these things. They know that the sportsmen and women, being the main attraction, take priority and have to be treated properly. They know too that winning is the biggest buzz of all, and no sport is worth a dime unless everybody is eyeballs-out "giving it heaps", as they like to put it. They also know that the fans are important, that they like to be comfortable and that the amber nectar has to be in plentiful supply. The Aussies have got it all worked out: playing sport is the most important thing in the world, partying comes second and talking sport a close third.

As a country they have got everything – golden beaches, wall-to-wall sunshine, wide open spaces, green valleys and hills. Settlers from five continents have added to the culture, ambience and cuisine over the years, so much so that Sydney and Melbourne are now among the most cosmopolitan cities on earth.

The outdoor culture is pervasive and stimulating. People live and play outdoors. No wonder they are so healthy. This is arguably the greatest sporting nation on earth, with sporting heroes wherever you look. Reigning world rugby champions, reigning world cricket champions, home to some of the world's greatest athletes and, in the case of Ian Thorpe, possibly the greatest swimmer the planet has ever known.

Some of the world's greatest-ever surfers come from Australia, while Oz has also spawned many tennis 'greats' such as Rod Laver, Lew Hoad and more recently Leyton Hewitt, as well as world-class sailors, netball and hockey players, and world-champion Formula One drivers. It is the home of Olympic 400m champion Kathy Freeman, venue for the Melbourne Cup horse race every November – and, heck, they even beat England at football these days.

All this variety is in a country whose two main sports, historically, are Rugby League and Australian Rules Football games, which scarcely register on the world scene. If the brilliant athletes who concentrate on those two sports ever diversified, it's frightening to think how good, or rather how much better, Australia might become in other spheres.

A pantheon of world sports

Given Australia's passion for sport, it was no surprise to anybody that they hosted the greatest Olympics ever, in Sydney in 2000, an event which virtually saved the Olympic movement after the farce of Atlanta 96. The Rugby World Cup, we are told, ranks third only behind the Olympics and the Football World Cup in the pantheon of world sporting events, so expect all the expertise and experience gained three years ago to come into play as the Aussies organize this seven-week extravaganza of rugby.

The stadia will be excellent, starting with Stadium Australia, which featured so prominently in the Olympics. The Colonial Stadium, Melbourne, with its state-of-the-art retractable roof, and the SunCorp Stadium in Brisbane are both magnificent 50,000-plus capacity sporting arenas, while there will also be a chance to watch rugby outside of the major hotspots – Townsville up in sweltering northern Queensland and Launceston, previously virgin territory as far as rugby is concerned, way down south in Tasmania.

The Australian authorities have deliberately taken the World Cup around the country, and only the remote Northern Territories will miss out. There will be 11 venues, in 10 cities. The purpose of the exercise is twofold. Firstly, to sell the game across the nation. For years Union was the poor cousin of League in Australia but on the back of two World Cup successes it has caught and now overtaken the 13-man game. The Australian Rugby Union is determined to build on that. Secondly, the Australians want you to see and fall in love with their country, which won't be at all difficult. Each Pool encompasses at least three locations and the fans will love the travelling around, the impromptu parties and getting that glorious sun on their backs.

There is so much to see. Sydney alone could keep you enchanted for months. There is also the New South Wales coast from Gosford northwards, genteel Adelaide, which will be making its debut as a rugby venue, while up in Queensland there's Brisbane, the Gold Coast and the Great Barrier Reef. Over in Western Australia Perth is blessed with the perfect climate and with some of the world's best beaches just around the corner, while Launceston and Tasmania have a charm all of their own.

It's all there to be enjoyed for the duration of the World Cup – and beyond for those who get the taste and immediately book next year's holiday. As Peter Dodds McCormick, who penned the Australian national anthem at the turn of the century, put it:

Australians all, let us rejoice,
For we are young and free;
We've golden soil and wealth for toil,
Our home is girt by sea;
Our land abounds in Nature's gifts
Of beauty rich and rare;
In history's page, let every stage
Advance Australia fair!

The Venues

Stadium Australia, Sydney: venue for athletics at the 200 Olympics and now the RWC 2003 Final.

Australian Capital Territory

Canberra
Canberra Stadium

Canberra Stadium, formerly known as Bruce Stadium, is the home ground of the ACT Brumbies Super 12 team and the Canberra Raiders National Rugby League Team. Built in 1977, the stadium has undergone a series of upgrades over the years and now boasts a capacity of 25,000. The stadium hosted soccer fixtures during the Sydney 2000 Olympic Games.

Matches

October 15:	**Italy v Tonga**
October 19:	**Wales v Tonga**
October 21:	**Italy v Canada**
October 25:	**Italy v Wales**

New South Wales

Sydney
Stadium Australia

Stadium Australia was the main venue for the Sydney 2000 Olympic and Paralympic Games, as well as hosting the Opening and Closing Ceremonies. A multi-purpose event venue, Stadium Australia was officially opened in 1999 and accommodated a world record 109,874 fans for the Australia v New Zealand Bledisloe Cup match in 2000. Following the Sydney 2000 Games, the capacity has been modified and will now be 80,000.

Matches

October 10:	**Australia v Argentina**
October 25:	**France v Scotland**
November 2:	**New Zealand v Wales**
November 15:	**Semi-final**
November 16:	**Semi-final**
November 20:	**3rd/4th play-off**
November 22:	**Final**

Sydney
Aussie Stadium

Aussie Stadium, the home ground of New South Wales Waratahs, was formerly Sydney Football Ground and totally separate from Stadium Australia. It was specifically built in 1988 as a multi-purpose football stadium and hosted Wallaby Test rugby matches in Sydney between 1989 and 1998 and was an Olympic Games soccer venue in 2000. The capacity is 42,000.

Matches

October 19:	**Ireland v Namibia**
October 22:	**Argentina v Romania**
October 24:	**South Africa v Georgia**
October 28:	**Georgia v Uruguay**
November 1:	**Scotland v Fiji**

Gosford
North Power Stadium

Located at Gosford on NSW's Central Coast, **North Power Stadium** has a capacity of 20,000 and was built on the site of Grahame Park. It is one of the home grounds of National Rugby League club, the Northern Eagles. The stadium has also been a popular rugby venue and successfully hosted the British and Irish Lions match against Australia A in 2001.

Matches

October 11:	**Ireland v Romania**
October 14:	**Argentina v Namibia**
October 27:	**Japan v USA**

G'Day mate. Read the Ocker's guide yet?

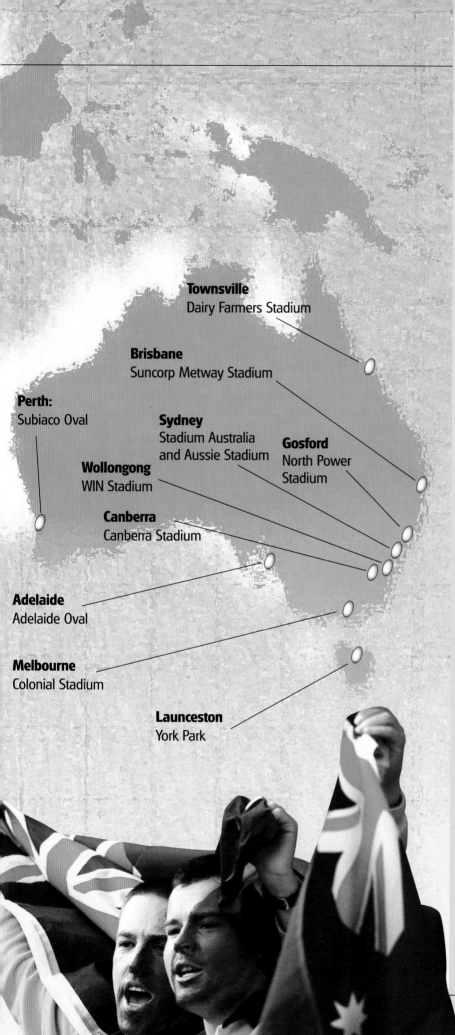

Townsville
Dairy Farmers Stadium

Brisbane
Suncorp Metway Stadium

Perth:
Subiaco Oval

Sydney
Stadium Australia
and Aussie Stadium

Gosford
North Power
Stadium

Wollongong
WIN Stadium

Canberra
Canberra Stadium

Adelaide
Adelaide Oval

Melbourne
Colonial Stadium

Launceston
York Park

Ocker's Guide

The Australians have developed their own very distinctive slang known as 'Strine. You'll quickly pick it up but here's a rough guide to get you started.

Aerial pingpong: Australian Rules Football

Ankle biter: small child

Arvo: afternoon

Aussie salute: brushing away flies with the hand

B & S: Bachelors' and Spinsters' Ball – a very enjoyable party usually held in rural areas

Back of Bourke: a very long way away

Banana bender: a person from Queensland

Bastard: term of endearment

Bingle: motor vehicle accident

Bloody oath: that's certainly true

Bludger: lazy person, layabout.

Blue: fight ("He was having a blue with his wife.")

Blue, make a: make a mistake

Bonzer: great (same as "ripper")

Boogie board: a hybrid, half-sized surf board

Booze bus: police vehicle used for catching drunk drivers

Brisvegas: Brisbane, state capital of Queensland

Brumby: a wild horse

Buck's night: stag party, male gathering the night before a wedding

Bundy: short for Bundaberg, Queensland, and the local rum

Bush telly: campfire

Butcher: small glass of beer in South Australia; from the theory that a butcher could take a quick break from his job, have a drink and be back at work

Chuck a sickie: take the day off sick from work when you're perfectly healthy

Clayton's: fake, substitute

Click: kilometre ("It's 10 clicks away.")

Cobber: friend

Cockroach: a person from New South Wales

Crack onto (someone): to hit on someone, pursue someone romantically

Crook: sick, or badly made

Crow-eater: a person from South Australia

Cut snake, mad as a: very angry

Dag: a funny person, nerd, goof

Daks: trousers

Dero: tramp, hobo, homeless person (from "derelict")

Digger: a soldier

Dill: an idiot

Dingo's breakfast: a yawn, a leak and a good look round (i.e. no breakfast)

Dole bludger: somebody on social assistance when unjustified

Drink with the flies: to drink alone

Dunny: outside lavatory

Dunny rat, cunning as a: very cunning

Durry: cigarette

Esky: large insulated food/drink container for picnics, barbecues, etc.

Face, off one's: drunk ("He was off his face by 9 pm.")

Feral: a hippie

Fisho: fishmonger

Flake: shark's flesh (sold in fish and chip shops)

Ocker's Guide

Flick: to give something or someone the flick is to get rid of it or him/her

Footy: Australian Rules Football

Fossick: to search, rummage; to prospect, e.g. for gold

Franger: condom

Fremantle doctor: the cooling afternoon breeze that arrives in Perth from the direction of Freeo

Frog in a sock, as cross as a: sounding angry – either a person or your hard drive!

Galah: fool, named after the bird of the same name, which flies south in the winter – a bloody silly thing to do in the southern hemisphere!

Going off: used of a night spot or party that is a lot of fun ("The place was really going off.")

Good oil: useful information, a good idea, the truth

Grinning like a shot fox: very happy, smugly satisfied

Grundies: undies, underwear (from Reg Grundy, a television person)

Hooroo: goodbye

Icy pole, ice block: popsicle, lollypop

Jackaroo: a male station hand (a station is a big farm/grazing property)

Jillaroo: a female station hand

Jumbuck: sheep

Kangaroos loose in the top paddock: intellectually inadequate ("He's got kangaroos loose in the top paddock.")

Kero: kerosene

Knock: to criticize

Knock back: refusal (noun), refuse (verb)

Larrikin: a bloke who is always enjoying himself, harmless prankster

Liquid laugh: vomit

Lizard drinking, flat out like a: flat out, busy

London to a brick: absolute certainty ("It's London to a brick that taxes won't go down.")

Long paddock: the side of the road where livestock is grazed during droughts

Lucky Country, The: Australia – where else?

Lurk: illegal or underhand racket

Maccas (pron. "mackers"): McDonald's (the hamburger place)

Mate's rate: cheaper than usual for a "friend"

Matilda: swagman's bedding, sleeping roll

Mexican: a person from south of the (Queensland) border

Middy: 285ml beer glass in New South Wales

Milko: milkman

Moolah: money

Mozzie: mosquito

Muddy: mud crab (a great delicacy)

Nasho: National Service (compulsory military service)

Never Never: the Outback, centre of Australia

Nipper: young surf lifesaver

No worries!: expression of forgiveness or reassurance

Ocker: an unsophisticated person

Offsider: an assistant, helper

Oldies: parents

Pash: a long passionate kiss; hence "pashing on"

Perve (noun and verb): looking lustfully at the opposite sex

Melbourne's Colonial Stadium boasts a state-of-the-art retractable roof.

Wollongong
WIN Stadium

WIN Stadium is the Illawarra region home ground for St George-Illawarra National Rugby League team and National Soccer League champions, Wollongong Wolves. A new north stand was completed in 2002 and the stadium now has a capacity of 20,000.

Matches
October 29: **Canada v Tonga;**
October 31: **France v USA**

Queensland

Brisbane
Suncorp Metway Stadium

Suncorp Metway Stadium (formerly Lang Park) is currently undergoing major works and will enjoy a capacity of 52,500 for Rugby World Cup 2003. The Suncorp has hosted a number of rugby Tests, the most recent being the 1999 Tri-Nations match between Australia and South Africa.

Matches
October 15: **Fiji v USA**
October 18: **Australia v Romania**
October 20: **Scotland v USA**
October 24: **New Zealand v Tonga**
November 1: **South Africa v Samoa**
November 2: **England v Uruguay**
November 8: **Quarter-final 1**
November 9: **Quarter-final 2**

Townsville
Dairy Farmers Stadium

Located in northern Queensland, **Dairy Farmers Stadium** is the home ground of National Rugby League club, the North Queensland Cowboys. The 31,500 capacity venue hosted the tour match between the British & Irish Lions and the Queensland President's XV last year.

Matches
October 12: **Scotland v Japan**
October 18: **France v Japan**
October 23: **Fiji v Japan**

South Australia

Adelaide
Adelaide Oval

Adelaide Oval is one of the world's most picturesque cricket grounds. Home of the South Australian Redbacks cricket team, the 45,000 capacity Oval is also a popular venue for the South Australian National Football League. International rugby made its debut at the ground on June 18 when Australia A played France A.

Matches
October 25: **Australia v Namibia**
October 26: **Argentina v Ireland**

Tasmania

Launceston
York Park

York Park is a new venue for rugby. The ground, which has a capacity of 20,000, has recently undergone a major redevelopment. It plays host to the AFL club Hawthorn for three matches each AFL season and also hosts a team in the local Tasmanian Australian Football competition.

Matches
October 30: **Namibia v Romania**

Victoria

Melbourne
Colonial Stadium

The 52,000 capacity **Colonial Stadium** is Melbourne's newest international events venue. With a roof that can be closed when required, Colonial Stadium hosted the first-ever indoor rugby Test when Australia played South Africa for the Nelson Mandela Challenge Plate in 2000. Colonial Stadium is also the home ground to a number of Melbourne-based Australian Football League teams.

Matches
October 11: **New Zealand v Italy**
October 12: **Wales v Canada**
October 17: **New Zealand v Canada**
October 26: **England v Samoa**
November 1: **Australia v Ireland**
November 8: **Quarter-final 1**
November 9: **Quarter-final 2**

Western Australia

Perth
Subiaco Oval

Situated in Perth, **Subiaco Oval** is the home of Australian Football League teams, West Coast Eagles and the Fremantle Dockers. It has been a regular Test rugby venue in recent years following the first-ever Test at the ground in 1998. Subiaco now has a capacity of 43,000 following a major redevelopment.

Matches
October 11: **South Africa v Uruguay**
October 12: **England v Georgia**
October 15: **Samoa v Uruguay**
October 18: **South Africa v England**
October 19: **Georgia v Samoa**

Ocker's Guide

Pig's arse!: I don't agree with you

Pokies: poker machines, fruit machines, gambling slot machines

Pommy bastard: an Englishman

Pommy shower: using deodorant instead of taking a shower

Pommy's towel, as dry as a: very dry – based on the belief that Poms bathe about once a month

Pot: 285ml beer glass in Queensland and Victoria

Quid, make a: earn a living ("Are you making a quid?")

Quid, not the full: of low IQ

Raw prawn, to come the: to bullshit, to be generally disagreeable

Ripper: great, fantastic ("It was a ripper party!")

Road train: big truck with many trailers

Roo: kangaroo

Salvos, the: Salvation Army, bless them

Sandgroper: a person from Western Australia

Schooner: large beer glass in Queensland; medium beer glass in South Australia

Seppo: an American

Shark biscuit: somebody new to surfing

Sheila: a woman

Skull/Skol (a beer): to drink a beer in a single draught without taking a breath

Slab: a carton of 24 bottles or cans of beer

Smoko: smoke or coffee break

Stoked: very pleased

Strides: trousers

Strine: Australian slang and pronunciation

Stubby: a 375ml beer bottle

Swag: rolled-up bedding, etc. carried by a swagman

Tall poppies: successful people

Tallie: 750ml bottle of beer

Taswegian: a person from Tasmania

Technicolor yawn: vomit

Tinny: can of beer

Togs: swimsuit

Troppo, gone: to have escaped to a state of tropical madness

Tucker: food

Turps, hit the: go on a drinking binge

Two up: gambling game played by spinning two coins simultaneously

Up oneself: have a high opinion of oneself ("He's really up himself.")

Useful as an ashtray on a motorbike: unhelpful or incompetent person or thing

Vee dub: Volkswagen

Veg out: relax in front of the TV (like a vegetable)

Walkabout: a walk in the Outback by Aborigines that lasts for an indefinite amount of time

Whacker, whacka: idiot; somebody who talks drivel; somebody with whom you have little patience.

Wobbly boot on, he's got the: drunk

Woop Woop: invented name for any small, unimportant town

Wowser: straight-laced person, prude, puritan, spoilsport

Yakka: work (noun)

Zack: sixpence, or 5 cents ("It isn't worth a zack.")

The Road to Oz
Qualifying for the World Cup

While all eyes focus on Australia this October and November, it is perhaps interesting to ponder the fact that the 2003 World Cup is already 75 per cent over. The qualification process was long and hard but immensely enjoyable and served its own purpose. The vast majority of the world's 92 rugby-playing nations do not have a Six Nations or Tri-Nations competition in their calendar, so the World Cup qualifying rounds are their competitive focus and the highlight of their season.

It also gives the loyal local sponsors their day in the spotlight, with the publicity and kudos of staging a World Cup match. The vast majority of the teams know they have no chance of qualifying but that doesn't stop them relishing the challenge.

In the RWC 2003 qualifying process there

have been no major surprises but a lot of good rugby and fun. The process started back in 2001 with 12 places up for grabs; the other eight places were pre-allocated to the eight quarter-finalists from RWC 1999 – Wales, Scotland, England, France, Argentina, Australia, New Zealand and South Africa.

Europe

In Europe these days the net is being spread ever wider in the early rounds, with Malta and Monaco making their debut alongside the likes of Lithuania, Slovenia, Moldova, Andorra and Bosnia. By Round Three the Czech Republic and Poland had emerged to challenge the more established countries and, although neither made it through to the decisive Round Four, their appearance in the latter stages of the qualifying process offers encouraging evidence of their progress.

In the final dust-up, in Round Four, it was Russia and Georgia who took on Ireland, and Spain and Romania who challenged Italy, with the top two in each mini-pool earning certain qualification.

The Russian Pool featured an historic first visit by Ireland to Krasnoyarsk in Siberia where they won 35–3 in one of the great rugby adventures of recent times. Ireland chartered their own plane, stayed on Irish time for the 84-hour long weekend, despite crossing and re-crossing 16 separate time zones, and encountered 80-degree heat rather than the expected freezing conditions as they sampled life on the road Russian style. They also experienced heart-warming, traditional rugby hospitality from a remote area of the earth where rugby burns bright. Krasnoyarsk boasts Russia's top two club teams and an extraordinary crowd of 25,000 turned up to support their team.

The match was brilliantly staged, with dual-language programmes and announcements. The Russian side wasn't bad either and it was possible to see rugby's massive potential in this country, which made the team's subsequent expulsion from the repechage round against Spain for fielding illegal players all the more disappointing.

The Russians were found guilty of fielding three South Africa-reared players who could not provide the documentary evidence of their Russian heritage – they claimed to have Russian grandfathers when in fact it was clear that great-grandfather was the likely relationship. The Spanish blew the whistle on them and the Russians were kicked out,

O'Driscoll in action.

a harsh lesson especially when you consider some of the dubious claims to nationality we have witnessed in other more established countries.

Ireland went on to defeat Georgia comprehensively in Dublin, but the former Russian state were saving their major effort to defeat Russia in Tblisi in order to clinch qualification. This they duly did, 17–13, in front of an unusually small 30,000 crowd – a serious security alert before the game meant that thousands of supporters were left outside the ground.

In the second pool, with new coach John Kirwan beginning to feel his way, Italy won impressively away to Spain but, after choosing to rest some of their senior players, were hard pressed by a much-improved Romania, who also booked their ticket to Australia.

Africa

In the African group, meanwhile, only one automatic place was up for grabs and after the early rounds, in which Madagascar made an impression for the first time, it came down to a double-header play-off between Namibia, who qualified, from the South, and the rapidly improving Tunisians from North Africa.

Everybody assumed that Namibia's superior power up front would be decisive but a couple of their more experienced players based in South Africa were unavailable and it was by no means plain sailing in the first leg at Windhoek, Namibia winning 26–19. The Namibians approached the return leg with some trepidation and started to get edgy when they were mysteriously delayed for over two hours by immigration at a sweltering Tunis airport and a noisy mob appeared outside their hotel late on the eve of the game.

On the pitch, life was just as tough and the Tunisians, who have learned their rugby from the French and like to attack and handle in the French style, emerged as 24–17 winners. The play-off therefore was

tied 43–43 and Namibia only progressed by virtue of having scored one more try.

Asia

No such excitement over in Asia where Japan absolutely blitzed their way through the final qualification pool, defeating Taiwan 155–3 and 120–3 and then dishing out 90–24 and 55–17 drubbings to old rivals Korea. Either Japan have improved dramatically – which is possible, they do finally seem to be fulfilling their potential – or standards in Asia are slipping alarmingly. There was a time when Korea looked capable of making a breakthrough internationally but their decline was further emphasized when they were outclassed in the repechage, conceding 194 points against Tonga and failing to score themselves.

Oceania

In the Oceanic group, it is always a matter of who secures automatic qualification out of the old island rivals Fiji, Tonga and Samoa. This time it was the Fijians and Samoans, but Tonga made light of their repechage duties, crushing Papua New Guinea and Korea, using the trips as training camps and introducing a number of promising players.

In the earlier rounds in this section we saw the World Cup debut of what is probably the world's smallest rugby-playing nation, Niue Island, who by no means disgraced themselves in losing to the Cook Islands in their first game and then recorded a famous win over Tahiti. Later in the year they became the most popular minnows in the Commonwealth Games Sevens tournament in Manchester.

America

Finally, the America Group went right down to the wire

with all four teams in the last section – Canada, USA, Uruguay and Chile – going into the final weekend with chances of making qualification. In the event, it was Canada and Uruguay who prevailed, the latter making the finals for the second consecutive tournament. USA will have been disappointed at having to enter Australia via the back door, i.e. the repechage system, while Chile must be encouraged by their continued development as the South American region is becoming increasingly competitive.

Fiji's Simon Raiwalui wins the line-out ball.

EUROPE

ROUND ONE

POOL A

Monaco	15	Moldova	17
Belgium	24	Slovenia	10
Slovenia	19	Lithuania	19
Moldova	58	Malta	8
Malta	0	Belgium	26
Monaco	8	Slovenia	13
Malta	3	Monaco	9
Monaco	12	Belgium	18
Belgium	26	Moldova	10
Malta	11	Lithuania	39
Slovenia	30	Moldova	15
Belgium	29	Lithuania	20
Slovenia	45	Malta	5
Lithuania	33	Monaco	10
Moldova	20	Lithuania	16

POOL B

Bosnia	13	Hungary	12
Switzerland	43	Bosnia	6
Andorra	12	Yugoslavia	9
Bulgaria	9	Switzerland	90
Hungary	27	Andorra	21
Yugoslavia	46	Bulgaria	6
Yugoslavia	25	Hungary	10
Switzerland	38	Andorra	25
Bulgaria	30	Bosnia	8
Switzerland	61	Hungary	23
Bosnia	23	Yugoslavia	13
Andorra	59	Bulgaria	10
Hungary	46	Bulgaria	7
Yugoslavia	13	Switzerland	10
Andorra	23	Bosnia	13

POOL C

Norway	9	Luxembourg	41
Austria	10	Sweden	42
Latvia	24	Luxembourg	19
Sweden	44	Norway	3
Latvia	38	Austria	12
Luxembourg	3	Israel	62
Israel	3	Latvia	21
Israel	43	Norway	3
Luxembourg	3S	Sweden	116
Austria	77	Luxembourg	0
Sweden	35	Israel	20
Latvia	37	Norway	0
Austria	21	Israel	6
Norway	7	Austria	51
Sweden	17	Latvia	10

ROUND TWO

POOL A

Czech Rep.	46	Belgium	3
Switzerland	6	Czech Rep.	32
Croatia	5	Czech Rep.	13
Ukraine	21	Belgium	10
Ukraine	34	Croatia	7
Belgium	15	Switzerland	22
Czech Rep.	26	Ukraine	8
Croatia	18	Switzerland	16
Switzerland	11	Ukraine	30
Belgium	0	Croatia	26

POOL B

Latvia	8	Poland	60
Poland	18	Sweden	6
Sweden	37	Latvia	12
Sweden	32	Germany	10
Denmark	33	Sweden	21
Denmark	19	Poland	26
Germany	34	Denmark	24
Germany	44	Latvia	0
Latvia	8	Denmark	32
Poland	20	Germany	12

ROUND THREE

POOL A

Czech Rep.	18	Russia	37
Netherlands	12	Czech Rep.	54
Russia	65	Netherlands	3

POOL B

Poland	27	Spain	15
Portugal	39	Poland	26
Spain	34	Portugal	21

ROUND FOUR

POOL 1

Russia	3	Ireland	35
Ireland	63	Georgia	14
Georgia	17	Russia	3

POOL 2

Spain	3	Italy	50
Italy	25	Romania	17
Romania	67	Spain	6

Ireland, Georgia, Italy and Romania qualify automatically for the World Cup Finals. Russia and Spain go into the repechage.

OCEANIA

ROUND ONE

EASTERN ZONE

Cook Islands	86	Tahiti	0
Niue Island	8	Cook Islands	28
Tahiti	6	Niue Island	41

WESTERN ZONE

Papua New Guinea	32	Solomon Islands	10
Vanuatu	10	Papua New Guinea	32
Solomon Islands	11	Vanuatu	3

ROUND TWO

Samoa	16	Fiji	17
Tonga	22	Fiji	47
Tonga	16	Samoa	25
Samoa	31	Tonga	13
Fiji	47	Tonga	20

Samoa and Fiji qualify automatically for Australia.

ROUND THREE

Papua New Guinea	29	Cook Islands	14
Cook Islands	21	Papua New Guinea	16

PNG win 42–35 on aggregate.

REPECHAGE

Papua New Guinea	14	Tonga	47
Tonga	84	Papua New Guinea	12

Tonga go into repechage.

Namibia v Tunisia in a qualifying game.

AFRICA

ROUND ONE

POOL A

Zambia	25	Cameroon	24
Uganda	21	Zambia	12
Cameroon	17	Uganda	0

POOL B

Botswana	13	Swaziland	3
Madagascar	31	Botswana	11
Swaziland	21	Madagascar	26

ROUND TWO

Madagascar	27	Kenya	20
Cameroon	24	Madagascar	30
Kenya	40	Cameroon	15

ROUND THREE

POOL A

Tunisia	27	Morocco	26
Côte d'Ivoire	8	Tunisia	13
Morocco	23	Côte d'Ivoire	21

POOL B

Madagascar	3	Zimbabwe	52
Namibia	116	Madagascar	0
Zimbabwe	30	Namibia	42

ROUND FOUR

Namibia	26	Tunisia	19
Tunisia	24	Namibia	17

Aggregate tied on 43–43.

Namibia qualify by virtue of scoring more tries. Tunisia go into the repechage system.

AMERICAS

ROUND ONE

NORTH

Bahamas	18	Barbados	2
Trinidad & Tobago	51	Jamaica	5
Caymen Islands	32	Guyana	13
Bermuda	13	Barbados	5
Trinidad & Tobago	12	Caymen Islands	8
Bermuda	12	Trinidad & Tobago	23

SOUTH

Venezuela	55	Colombia	0
Venezuela	46	Peru	19
Brazil	51	Peru	9
Colombia	12	Brazil	47
Brazil	14	Venezuela	3
Peru	31	Colombia	10

ROUND TWO

Trinidad & Tobago	10	Brazil	11
Brazil	9	Trinidad & Tobago	0

Brazil win 30–10 on aggregate.

ROUND THREE

Brazil	6	Chile	46
Paraguay	14	Brazil	13
Chile	57	Paraguay	5

ROUND FOUR

Canada	26	USA	9
USA	13	Canada	36
Chile	10	Uruguay	6
Canada	51	Uruguay	16
USA	35	Chile	22
USA	28	Uruguay	24
Canada	27	Chile	6
Chile	21	USA	13
Uruguay	25	Canada	23
Chile	11	Canada	29
Uruguay	10	USA	9
Uruguay	34	Chile	23

Canada and Uruguay qualify, USA go into the repechage.

ASIA

ROUND ONE

POOL 1

Malaysia	3	Taiwan	57
Singapore	34	Malaysia	5I
Taiwan w/o Singapore			

POOL 2

Arabian Gulf	40	Thailand	20
Thailand	8	Hong Kong	15
Hong Kong	17	Arabian Gulf	7

POOL 3

Sri Lanka	9	China	7
China	57	Kazakhstan	15
Kazakhstan	24	Sri Lanka	14

ROUND TWO

Taiwan	20	Hong Kong	15
China	21	Taiwan	29
Hong Kong	34	China	7

ROUND THREE

Japan	90	Korea	24
Taiwan	31	Korea	54
Korea	119	Taiwan	7
Japan	155	Taiwan	3
Korea	17	Japan	55
Taiwan	3	Japan	120

Japan qualify, Korea go into the repechage.

REPECHAGE ONE

Korea	0	Tonga	75
Tonga	119	Korea	0

Tonga win 194–0 on aggregate.
Tonga qualify for Australia.

REPECHAGE TWO

Spain	33	Tunisia	16

Spain move forward to meet USA.

Spain	13	USA	62
USA	58	Spain	13

USA win 120–26 on aggregate. USA qualify.

N.B. Russia had originally beaten Spain 58–41 on aggregate but were expelled from competition for fielding ineligible players.

Tournament Preview

So who is going to win the 2003 Rugby World Cup? It's the question that intrigues every rugby fan and the good news for the neutral is that, although most of the bookies agree England are the favourites, it would also appear to be the most open competition to date.

A few general guidelines first. In three of the four tournaments to date, the host nation has either won the competition (New Zealand in 1987, South Africa in 1995) or reached the final (England in 1991). Only Wales in 1999 failed to reach the final, losing to eventual winners Australia in the quarter-finals. Home advantage therefore is a huge factor, as it was in the Football World Cup last year when Japan and South Korea performed well above expectations.

There are a couple of other general trends to note. Thus far only three countries have won the competition – New Zealand, South Africa and Australia (twice) – with the southern hemisphere totally dominant. On top of that, no side has ever retained the William Webb Ellis Trophy.

Playing conditions will be important. The tournament will be played early in the summer and conditions underfoot should be nigh on perfect, with hard grounds definitely favouring the athletic top-of-the surface teams and those who enjoy the handling game. It's going to be hot – all the time up in Brisbane and Townsville and most of the time everywhere else.

Former Australian captain John Eales, who led his side to victory last time out, believes the heat will be a bigger factor than many people realize.

"October and November are not normally rugby months in Australia, our domestic season is usually well wrapped up by then," says Eales. "Most of the time conditions will be superb but sides have got to be ready for sudden extreme heat and prepare accordingly. By the knock-out stages in November, at any of the venues, it would be no surprise if we suddenly hit a very warm spell and the temperatures soar to nearly 100°F."

THE POOLS

Pool A:
Australia (1), Argentina (8), Ireland, Namibia, Romania

Pool B:
France (2), Scotland (7), Fiji, Japan, USA

Pool C:
South Africa (3), England (6), Samoa, Uruguay, Georgia

Pool D:
New Zealand (4), Wales (5), Italy, Canada, Tonga

(Numbers in brackets denote seeded teams.)

POOL A

On paper, Pool A looks like the toughest pool in that it contains three teams – Australia, Argentina and Ireland – who are all potential semi-finalists or better. This situation has arisen because Ireland, who have improved immeasurably in the last four years, failed to qualify for the quarter-finals in 1999 and were not, therefore, among the top eight seeds this time around. The competition is therefore going to be brutal and the introduction of bonus points for four or more tries scored in a game, or for losing by less than a given number of points, will mean that the big three will also have to be flat out against the two minnows – Namibia and Romania.

The opening game of the entire tournament should be a massive encounter, with Australia tackling Argentina. Although home advantage is a huge factor for the Australians, the nerves surrounding the home game can often inhibit the host nation and the Pumas are among the strongest and most cussed opponents you could ever encounter on such an occasion. All of Australia will heave a huge sigh of relief if they can start proceedings with a win.

Assuming no slip-ups against Romania and Namibia, the other two vital games will feature Ireland against Argentina at the Adelaide Oval on Sunday, October 26 and Ireland's clash with the Australians at the Colonial Stadium Melbourne on November 1. With the enormous first and second generation Irish population throughout Australia, both matches should generate a wonderful atmosphere and be showpiece occasions.

For Romania and Namibia the 'big one' will be at Launceston on October 30, the first rugby match of any note to be staged in Tasmania – an excellent opportunity for rugby to sell itself in a new area and for the good citizens of Launceston to join the party.

The Pool winners will play the runners-up of Pool B in their quarter-final at Brisbane, while the runners-up will play the winners of Pool B at the Colonial Stadium Melbourne.

PREDICTION

Pool winners: **Australia.**
Runners-up: **Ireland.**

POOL B

Two-times finalists France are clear favourites to win this pool but the race to be runners-up could be interesting, with Scotland possibly having the edge over the enigmatic Fijians, improving Japan and the physical Americans.

France are not traditionally the greatest

of starters in the World Cup but need to hit the ground running this time around against Fiji. The Fijians deserved to beat them in their pool game four years ago in Toulouse and were only denied by a couple of crass refereeing decisions.

The Fijians should enjoy the heat and humidity they expect to encounter but equally France will appreciate the dry, hard ground. It should be a spectacular game but France know what is coming and will be fully prepared.

The Scots open up against Japan at Townsville and should be prepared for an infinitely stronger and more physical Japan side than they have encountered in former years. They should also be prepared for a high level of support for the Japanese, with a large ex-patriot Japanese population now living in Queensland .

Scotland's game against Fiji in Townsville could be another crucial encounter and a potential banana skin for the Scots but, if all goes to plan, the Pool decider should see France play Scotland at Stadium Australia on October 25. France won

their most recent Six Nations encounter with laughable ease in Paris, cantering to a 38–3 win, but Scotland tend to be a much tougher proposition come World Cup time.

In the quarter-finals the Pool winners will meet the runners up of Pool A in Melbourne, while the Pool runners-up will play the winners of Pool A in Brisbane.

PREDICTION

Pool winners: **France.**
Runners-up: **Scotland.**

Far left: **South Africa's Corne Krige tackles Daniel Herbert of New Zealand.**

Left: **Simon Taylor of Scotland is tackled by François Gelez of France.**

POOL C

This is the easiest Pool to predict but also the Pool that features the biggest game of the early stages, England's clash with South Africa at Perth on October 18. With all due respect to Uruguay, Georgia and the ever-physical and popular Samoans, we already know which two teams will progress. The only question is in which order.

England are pre-tournament favourites, having defeated New Zealand, Australia and South Africa in their November friendlies, and inflicted defeats on France and Ireland en route to their Grand Slam in the spring. They are the form side, having recorded recent victories over every major rugby nation and possessing great strength in depth, except possibly at fly-half where Charlie Hodgson is so important.

They will, however, encounter an entirely different South Africa from the Springboks side they humiliated at Twickenham when they posted a record 52–3 win over the visitors. The South African tour party had fallen apart and were severly depleted by injuries. They will never play that badly again.

Subsequently a great rugby nation has been mobilizing all its forces to uncover new talent while a number of players on the verge of retirement have postponed their decision. Expect a mighty effort from the Boks in a city with a huge ex-patriot population of South Africans.

The prize for winning the match in Perth, and the Pool, is huge. The winners will play the runners up of Pool D – in realistic terms, either Wales, Italy or Canada. Neither England nor South Africa will fear them as quarter-final opponents. The losers, however, will face the winners of Pool D and you can put your life savings on that being New Zealand. Meeting the All Blacks in a World Cup quarter-final is the game that everybody wants to avoid.

PREDICTION
Pool winners: **England.**
Runners-up: **South Africa.**

POOL D

New Zealand are odds-on to win this pool at a canter and all the interest will feature on a terrific dust-up for the runners-up spot, with all four remaining teams – Italy, Wales, Canada and Tonga – having realistic chances.

As the second seeded team in the pool, Wales have the advantage of playing their three relevant games straight off – their concluding game against New Zealand will mean nothing, the All Blacks will have won the Pool and Wales will either have finished second or not. It means they can concentrate their effort fully on their first three games and their cause has again been helped by an extremely favourable draw.

Wales start against the Canadians, who invariably raise their game every four years for the World Cup. They then enjoy a full week's rest before tackling Tonga and another five days' break before the possibly decisive game against Italy in Canberra on October 25.

The Italians start against Tonga, have a six-day break before playing Canada and then have just three days to prepare for the big game against Wales, a plainly unfair schedule that they have repeatedly tried to change. All the teams will be tired and sore by this stage of the tournament and Italy are entitled to as much rest as the Welsh.

Second place in this pool will go all the way down to the wire and such is the obvious disparity between New Zealand and the other sides that you will almost certainly see the other four sides fielding weakened teams against the All Blacks to conserve and protect their key players. This is the pool in which the bonus points system will also have

most effect, possibly making all the difference between finishing second or third.

The penalty, if you like, for New Zealand of having such a relatively simple pool is that as pool winners they will face a quarter-final against either England or South Africa, a little early in the tournament to be meeting such monumental opposition. The runners-up face the hapless prospect of, again, playing either South Africa or England.

PREDICTION
Pool winners: **New Zealand.**
Runners-up: **Wales.**

Du Preez Grobler of Namibia encounters Tunisian defence.

The Schedule

Friday, October 10

Pool A
Australia v Argentina
Stadium Australia, Sydney

Saturday, October 11

Pool A
Ireland v Romania
Gosford

Pool B:
France v Fiji
Brisbane

Pool C
South Africa v Uruguay
Perth

Pool D
New Zealand v Italy
Melbourne

Sunday, October 12

Pool B
Scotland v Japan
Townsville

Pool C
England v Georgia
Perth

Pool D
Wales v Canada
Melbourne

Tuesday, October 14

Pool A
Argentina v Namibia
Gosford

Wednesday, October 15

Pool B
Fiji v USA
Brisbane

Pool C
Samoa v Uruguay
Perth

Pool D
Italy v Tonga
Canberra

Friday, October 17

Pool D
New Zealand v Canada
Melbourne

Saturday, October 18

Pool A
Australia v Romania
Brisbane

Pool B
France v Japan
Townsville

Pool C
South Africa v England
Perth

Sunday, October 19

Pool A
Ireland v Namibia
Aussie Stadium, Sydney

Pool C
Georgia v Samoa
Perth

Pool D
Wales v Tonga
Canberra

Monday, October 20

Pool B
Scotland v USA
Brisbane

Tuesday, October 21

Pool D
Italy v Canada
Canberra

Wednesday, October 22

Pool A
Argentina v Romania
Aussie Stadium, Sydney

Thursday, October 23

Pool B
Fiji v Japan
Townsville

Friday, October 24

Pool C
South Africa v Georgia
Aussie Stadium, Sydney

Pool D
New Zealand v Tonga
Brisbane

Saturday, October 25

Pool A
Australia v Namibia
Adelaide Oval

Pool B
France v Scotland
Stadium Australia, Sydney

Pool D
Italy v Wales
Canberra

Sunday, October 26

Pool A
Argentina v Ireland
Adelaide

Pool C
England v Samoa
Melbourne

Monday, October 27

Pool B
Japan v USA
Gosford

Tuesday, October 28

Pool C
Georgia v Uruguay
Aussie Stadium, Sydney

Wednesday, October 29

Pool D
Canada v Tonga
Wollongong

Thursday, October 30

Pool A
Namibia v Romania
York Park, Launceston

Friday, October 31

Pool B
France v USA
Wollongong

Saturday, November 1

Pool A
Australia v Ireland
Melbourne

Pool B
Scotland v Fiji
Aussie Stadium, Sydney

Pool C
South Africa v Samoa
Brisbane

Sunday, November 2

Pool C
England v Uruguay
Brisbane

Pool D
New Zealand v Wales
Stadium Australia, Sydney

Saturday, November 8

Quarter-finals

Winner Pool D v Runner-up Pool C
Melbourne

Winner Pool A v Runner-up Pool B
Brisbane

Sunday, November 9

Quarter-finals

Winner Pool B v Runner-up Pool A
Melbourne

Winner Pool C v Runner-up Pool D
Brisbane

Saturday, November 15

Semi-finals

Winner QF1 v Winner QF2
Stadium Australia, Sydney

Sunday, November 16

Semi-finals

Winner QF3 v Winner QF4
Stadium Australia, Sydney

Thursday, November 20

Play-off

Loser SF1 v Loser SF2
Stadium Australia, Sydney

Saturday, November 22

Final

Winner SF1 v Winner SF2
Stadium Australia, Sydney

Jonah Lomu brushes
Rob Andrews aside
and scores another
try for the All Blacks.

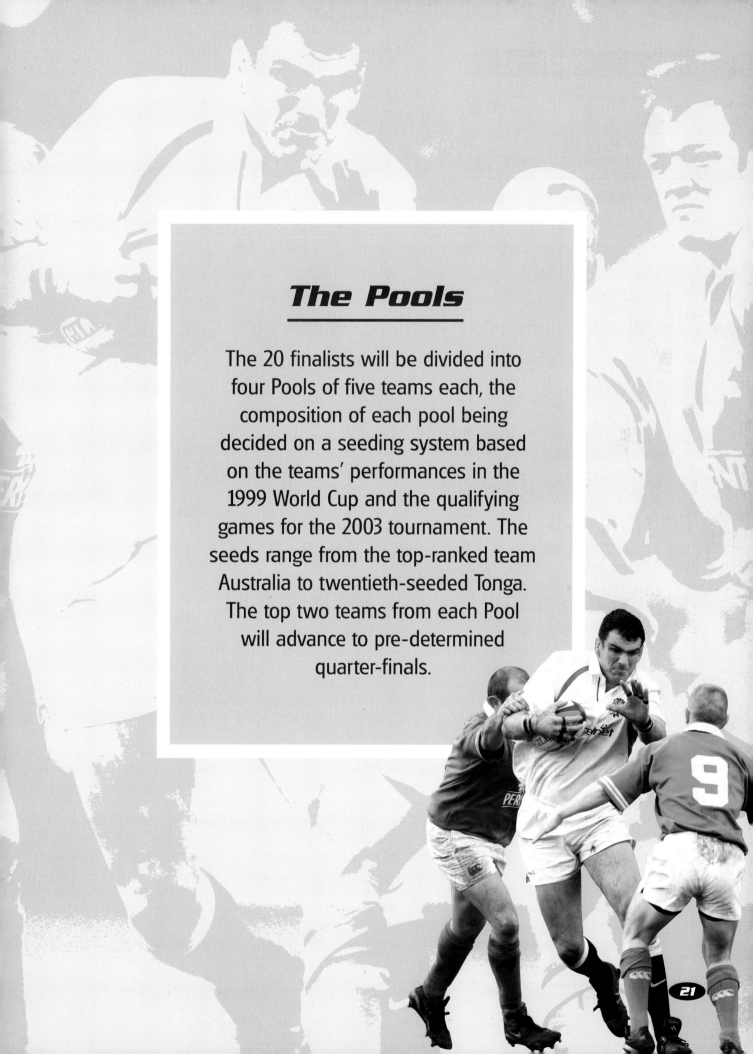

The Pools

The 20 finalists will be divided into four Pools of five teams each, the composition of each pool being decided on a seeding system based on the teams' performances in the 1999 World Cup and the qualifying games for the 2003 tournament. The seeds range from the top-ranked team Australia to twentieth-seeded Tonga. The top two teams from each Pool will advance to pre-determined quarter-finals.

Australia

The **Aussies** may have wobbled a little on their tour of Europe last autumn, losing to Ireland and England, but the reigning World Champions will be nothing less than formidable on their own turf.

Powerhouse centre Daniel Herbert in typical action.

Team Name	
The Wallabies	

Playing Strip
Gold jerseys, dark green shorts

Website
www.rugby.com.au

World Cup Record
1987: Semi-finalists
1991: Winners
1995: Quarter-finalists
1999: Winners

With the success of the Sydney Olympics still reverberating around the sporting world, they will be determined to put on another show and now that rugby union has finally secured its own important niche in the Australian sporting pantheon, the entire nation will be backing them. Frankly, it will be a surprise if they don't reach the final and if they do that you wouldn't bet against them.

They'll have to work hard, though, because the rather strange World Cup seeding system has placed them in one of the tougher pools alongside Argentina and Ireland, who are probably the two fastest improving sides in world rugby. All three

sides are potential semi-finalists, yet only two can progress to the knock-out stages, so Australia can afford no slip-ups. They have to hit the ground running.

The players

The strengths of the Australian side haven't changed from four years ago – supremely fit, well-organized defence, loads of experience in key positions, especially in the backs, and the ability not to concede too many penalties.

Captain George Gregan and fly-half Stephen Larkham are among the international game's most experienced and talented half-back combinations, though

the latter has been prone to injury problems in recent seasons. The blockbusting Daniel Herbert is still a tower of strength at centre and Matt Burke remains the most solid of full-backs as well as an ultra-reliable goal-kicker. Wing Joe Roff seems to have been around forever but is still well under 30 and, after a year's sabbatical from the international scene playing for Biarritz in France, looks refreshed and rejuvenated.

Of the younger generation, Chris Latham and Stirling Mortlock seem certain to feature prominently, but, alas, the long-striding Queensland wing Ben Tune will miss out after yet another serious knee injury. Rugby League import Mat Rogers has already made an impact, while Wendell Sailor shows signs of successfully making the transition too.

Up front, the back row has always been key, with George Smith one of the most mobile and effective tearaways and Owen Finegan, who will have to prove his fitness

Ruck and Maul

There are around 60 million kangaroos in Australia – that's three for every human.

Songs
"Advance Australia Fair" (national anthem)
"Waltzing Matilda"

Half-time Tipple
Castlemaine XXXX
A robust beer, of around 5.0 per cent ABV, an ice-cold XXXX is essential for rugby viewers down under. You'll have a "G'day" with a pack of these cool tubes.

after major shoulder injury, an old-style hard man and enforcer on the blind side. Slotting in at No. 8 is Toutai Kefu, one of the most powerful "hard yards" runners in world rugby. Kefu is one of four rugby-playing brothers from the Souths club in Brisbane and his father played in the Tonga side that famously defeated Australia in 1973. Nobody has yet truly replaced John Eales at lock but Justin Harrison and Nathan Strange are coming on well, while the front row, though not often earning the plaudits, rarely comes off second best.

Australia's World Cup history

Despite their recent success in the Tri-Nations and their five-year ownership of the Bledisloe Cup, the emergence of Australia as a rugby union superpower is comparatively recent. The Wallabies "golden era" began in 1991, when Nick Farr-Jones led the team, which included a young John Eales, to victory in the World Cup Final against England at Twickenham.

In 1997, when Rod Macqueen was appointed as the new Wallaby coach, no one could have predicted the unprecedented success that was to follow.

Australia have been blessed with some special players during that period but the real reason for Australia's success has been good old-fashioned hard work. In the boardroom, administration put in place structures to elevate the game to new levels. On the training paddock, innovations in technology, fitness and sports medicine have been fully utilized to prepare the Wallaby team.

The team has also displayed a remarkable composure. It is hard to remember any team in international rugby that has shown the composure to escape with more nail-biting victories. There was the extra-time victory over the Springboks in the 1999 Rugby World Cup semi-final, inspired by an extraordinary Larkham drop goal. Then there was John Eales' extra-time penalty goal to win the Tri Nations match against the All Blacks in Wellington in 2000, and more recently there was Toutai Kefu's remarkable try in the final seconds of the 2001 Bledisloe Test at Stadium Australia to send captain John Eales out on top. And who can forget Matthew Burke's extraordinary composure in the same match the next year, slotting the penalty goal that sealed the Bledisloe Cup for the fifth year in a row.

Australia have become a winning team, they have acquired the habit and it served them well in 1999 when they took the Webb Ellis Trophy in fine style, conceding just one try in the process.

One to Watch
George Gregan (scrum-half)

Nothing would be more appropriate at RWC 2003 than for Wallabies captain George Gregan to lead the host nation to victory. Gregan has been a massive figure for Australia ever since making his international debut against Italy in 1994. He is as fast and elusive as they come – as befits a former star of the Australia Sevens squad – and has a superb service. Gregan is also pound for pound probably Australia's strongest tackler. Along with the rest of the Australian squad he was disappointed with their showing in South Africa in 1995, but stormed back four years later when they took the Webb Ellis Trophy in Wales.

Argentina

Over the last four years, **Argentina** have developed into one of the most dangerous sides in world rugby, well capable of giving any of the elite nations a run for their money.

U nder coach Marcelo Loffreda, they have begun to trust, and use, their talented backs instead of relying totally on their mighty forwards who are still the best scrummagers in the world and whose upper-body strength saps the opposition in the tight encounters. In the last 18 months, apart from trouncing all opposition on the American continent, they have recorded victories on the road against Wales and Scotland, defeated the then reigning Grand Slam champions France in Buenos Aires, conceded second best to the All Blacks only in injury-time in a classic encounter at the famous River Plate Stadium and given world champions Australia a fright at home as well. They are improving by the year and, one day soon, are going to pull off a huge win in a big competition.

Argentina's commitment to the World Sevens series over the last four seasons has done much to ignite their back play and there is now a sense of adventure behind the scrum that never existed previously.

Rolando Martin, a veteran of numerous World Cup games.

The players

Full-back Ignacio Corleto, now starring for Stade Français, is one of the coming stars of world rugby, an attacker of pace, strength and vision. Corleto, a talented surfer who is looking forward to enjoying Australia's world-renowned breaks, is potentially one of the stars of the competition – Argentina must bring him into the game as much as possible.

Diego Albanese, currently plying his trade for Leeds in the Zurich Premiership, is

a supercharged competitor and it was his try that heralded the Pumas' famous World Cup play-off victory over Ireland four years ago. Captain Lisandro Arbizu is their midfield rock and he could be partnered by rising young star, Juan Martin Hernandez, another to emerge from Argentina's Sevens squad. His family have fond sporting memories of Australia – sister Maripi won an Olympic silver in the women's hockey at Sydney and two years later took gold in the world championship at Perth.

Fly-half Gonzalo Quesada is up there among the best goal-kickers in the world and was the leading points-scorer four

Team Name
Los Pumas
(The Pumas)

Playing Strip
Sky blue and white hooped jerseys, white shorts

Website
www.rugby.com.au

World Cup Record
1987: Pool
1991: Pool
1995: Pool
1999: Quarter-finalists

years ago with 103, but the new-look Argentina will probably go for the more attacking option of Felipe Contepomi. The latter is no mean goal-kicker himself though slightly less consistent than the metronomic Quesada. His twin brother, Manuel, is likely to feature in the squad as a wing and Argentinian critics reckon that his elder brother was the best of the lot before giving the game up to become a priest. Whoever appears at fly-half, he will undoubtedly be partnered, barring injury, by Agustin Pichot, a truly world-class scrum-half who any of the major rugby nations in the world would welcome into their squad. Pichot used to play his club rugby for Bristol and that week-in-week-out familiarity has served Argentina well.

Up front, you know that whoever appears in the Pumas front row will be top notch and their famous eight-man drive – the feared Bajada – is in full working order. Hooker Federico Mendez is respected throughout the world, while Mauricio Reggiardo is another fearsome scrummager, as is Roberto Grau. Perhaps the best of the lot is Omar Hasan, the cornerstone of Agen's mighty pack last season and a player who has impressed down under during a spell with ACT Brumbies. Hasan is an intriguing character who possesses a superb tenor voice and

Ruck and Maul

The recent economic crisis saw five presidents pass through the revolving door of government in a busy two weeks.

Song

"Himno Nacional Argentino"
(national anthem)

Half-time Tipple

Yerba Mate
Made from the leaves of a South American shrub, this warming "tea" has been popular for centuries in the rigorous climate of the Andes.

has been training for the last three years in France as an opera singer – he intends to turn professional as soon as his rugby career ends, possibly after the World Cup.

In the second row, the rising star is Rimas Alvarez, who has been making a huge impression for Perpignan in the French first division, while the back row is almost certain to feature the veteran Rolando Martin and the highly durable Santiago Phelan. The one to look out for here is Martin Durand, now 26 and anxious to make amends after missing the 1999 campaign through injury.

Argentina's World Cup history

For such a strong rugby nation, Argentina have not quite made the impact they should have in previous World Cups, though they have not always enjoyed the best of luck. In 1987 they claimed a solitary win, over Italy, but did not disgrace themselves against eventual winners New Zealand, losing 46–15. Four years later they did even better against the eventual winners, only losing 32–19 against Australia in a cracking encounter at Stradey Park but let themselves down in sloppy defeats to Wales and Western Samoa.

In 1995 they were again winless in a tough group featuring England, Samoa and Italy but four years ago they finally delivered, reaching the quarter-finals courtesy of that historic win at Lens and then going down with all guns blazing against France at Lansdowne Road.

This time around they again feature in the opening game of the tournament – against the Aussies. (In 1999 they played Wales first up at the Millennium Stadium.) Argentina will be right in the thick of it from the start, which is exactly how they like it!

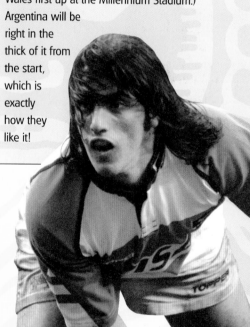

One to Watch

Agustin Pichot (scrum-half)

It is not just his long black hair and trademark headband that makes Agustin Pichot so easy to spot. The livewire Bristol scrum-half is invariably in the thick of the action, linking brilliantly with his forwards or using his exceptional pace to launch an attack of his own. Fiery and passionate, he has learned to curb his temperament a little in order to stop conceding needless penalties but he remains wholehearted and committed. Virtually ever-present since his debut in 1995, Pichot has also captained the Pumas Sevens team and is one of the most popular sportsmen in his country, wining the Sportsman of the Year award in 1999 ahead of various soccer stars, despite Argentina's excellent World Cup campaign.

Ireland

Ireland may have finished the Six Nations on a disappointing note with that 42–6 home defeat against a mighty England side but nothing can disguise the improvement they have made over the last two or three years.

Geordan Murphy on the run, chased by Italy's Alessandro Troncon and Aaron Persico.

Going into the England game they had won their previous ten internationals and for much of that time they had been suffering from an injury list as long as your arm, so if coach Eddie O'Sullivan can select from his full squad this autumn Ireland definitely have the potential to cause some damage.

They will, however, have to do it the hard way. Failure to reach the quarter-finals at the 1999 World Cup meant that not only did they have to qualify this time around but that they were not able to claim one of the top-eight seeded positions. The result is that they find themselves in a particularly tough group where there can be no slip-ups. Given Australia's home advantage it would be a major surprise if they defeated the Aussies – though that

possibility cannot be ruled out – but realistically their game against old adversaries Argentina at Adelaide on October 26 is the 'must-win' match if they are to advance to the quarter-finals.

The players

Eddie O'Sullivan has the raw material to work with. Geordan Murphy is a gem of a player, either at full-back or on the wing, and Ireland have got to find a way of bringing him into the game as often as possible. Girvan Dempsey is the safer option at full-back but a safety-first policy will win Ireland nothing. On the wings, Anthony Hogan and Shane Horgan should both have recovered from long-term injury and O'Sullivan will be hoping that Denis Hickie can rediscover some of the sparkle

that was missing from his play last season. Ulster's Tyronne Howe is another who might come into the reckoning.

At centre, the Brian O'Driscoll/Kevin Maggs axis is well established, but a return to full form and fitness by Rob Henderson, a Lion Down Under in 2001, will give O'Sullivan other options, and at fly-half the perennial vacillation between Ronan O'Gara and David Humphreys is set to continue. Peter Stringer is the first-choice scrum-half, though he needs to work a little on his pass, which has lost some of its snap. One of O'Sullivan's biggest problems is to find adequate back-up for Stringer – Llanelli's Guy Easterby is next in line, but after that there's a worrying void.

The Ireland pack in full cry is close to world class but too many matches and too many injuries eventually took their toll last season. Reinforcements are on the way,

Team Name
Ireland

Playing Strip
Emerald green jerseys, white shorts

Website
www.irishrugby.ie

World Cup Record
1987: Quarter-finalists
1991: Quarter-finalists
1995: 3rd
1999: Quarter-final
play-offs

Ruck and Maul

Dublin has become the stag and hen party capital of Europe.

Songs

"Soldiers Song"
(national anthem),
"Fields of Athenry",
"Molly Malone"

Half-time Tipple

Guinness
The black body and creamy white head of this unmistakable stout make Ireland's national drink recognized throughout the world. Just the stuff to kick you into touch!

though. The front row will be pepped up and strengthened by the return of Keith Wood, who is determined to end his career on a high note after a miserable year of injury, Paul Wallace and Reggie Corrigan, while athletic and aggressive young locks Donncha O'Callaghan and Paul O'Connell will be competing for a place in the second row alongside Malcolm O'Kelly, who has been in the form of his life.

Last season's established back row of No. 8 Anthony Foley and flankers Keith Gleeson and Victor Costello did well but the reappearance of a fully fit David Wallace and the return to form of Eric Miller and Kieron Dawson means, again, that Ireland should be able to mix and match depending on the opposition.

O'Sullivan and his management team are among the most thorough in the business so Ireland shouldn't miss a trick in that respect and, next to the home nation, they should be the best-supported side in the tournament with Australia being home to over a million people of Irish descent.

Ireland's World Cup history

The Irish have proved solid World Cup campaigners without ever quite reaching the heights. In 1987 they reached the quarter-finals comfortably enough before losing an exceptionally physical quarter-final against the Aussies, and four years later it was the same two sides that lined up at the same stage at Lansdowne Road. This time Ireland went into the lead with just three minutes left when Gordon Hamilton sprinted away for a try but Australia, like true champions, kept calm and stormed back to clinch the game with a try from Michael Lynagh.

In South Africa, Ireland went toe to toe with New Zealand and Jonah Lomu for well over an hour at Ellis Park before tiring in their pool game. However, they qualified for the quarter-finals by defeating Wales and Japan, although they got well beaten by France in Durban in the knock-out stages. 1999 was the big disappointment, when they came second in their pool to Australia and then lost to Argentina in the quarter-final play-offs, a game they seemed to be controlling midway through the second half. A quarter-final at Lansdowne Road against an out-of-sorts France had beckoned, but alas it was not to be – a golden opportunity missed.

One to Watch

Brian O'Driscoll (centre)

Everybody knows that Brian O'Driscoll is a danger man at centre but that doesn't necessarily make it any easier to stop him – O'Driscoll is already Ireland's leading try-scorer, passing Brendan Mullin's record of 17. Defences worked very hard to restrict him during Ireland's Six Nations campaign and to a certain extent were successful, but the time opponents spend concentrating on him usually frees up the likes of Geordan Murphy and others. He's learning to live with the extra attention opponents give him. Defensively O'Driscoll is rock solid, probably Ireland's hardest tackler, while his tactical kicking has improved considerably. A world-class player in his prime – the 2003 World Cup should provide the perfect stage to make an impact.

Namibia

With just 16 clubs in the country and under 600 senior players, **Namibia** have achieved a minor miracle simply by qualifying for RWC 2003 but, having earned their place in Australia, they are determined to make an impression.

Namibia has a proud rugby heritage and, before independence in 1990, competed in South Africa's Currie Cup regularly. Rugby is centred on the capital city of Windhoek where there is a strong club scene, though the game has never attracted the indigenous Africans or the large German population. Many of their best players, however, inevitably move to South Africa either to play or simply to complete their education or professional qualifications.

The players

Among Namibia's most highly rated players is scrum-half Hakkies Husselman who plays for Mpumulanga Pumas. Captain Corne Powell is a rock-solid centre from a big rugby-playing family – brothers Jimmy and Neil have both played for the Free State.

Powell is a GP, just like his fly-half Rudi van Vuuren who has also represented his country in the cricket World Cup in South Africa earlier this year.

Other players to watch are Brett Sparg, who plays his rugby for Saracens in England, and big lock Heino Senekal, a professional with Cardiff. Kees Lensing is a massive powerful prop with Eastern Province and Jurgen van Lills is an athletic No. 8 who has already attracted the attention of Western Province.

Coach David Waterston has a barrowload of experience, having acted as Kitch Christie's analyst both with the old Transvaal Currie Cup and Super Ten side and then the Springboks' 1995 World Cup-

winning squad. He also took Tonga to the 1999 finals and conjured up an impressive performance against New Zealand and a victory over Italy.

Namibia's World Cup history

Independence came too soon for Namibia to participate in 1991 – when ironically they had their strongest-ever side – and they failed to qualify in 1995. They did make it to the finals in 1999 but were generally outgunned, though a gutsy 47–13 defeat against France in Bordeaux hinted at their potential. Namibia qualified this year by the narrowest of margins, finishing level on aggregate at 43–43 apiece in their play-off double-header against Tunisia, only progressing by virtue of scoring one more try than their North African opponents.

Team Name
The Welwitschias*

Playing Strip
Sky blue, red and white jerseys, royal blue shorts

Website
www.geocities.com/VNamRugby

World Cup Record
1987: Did not qualify
1991: Did not qualify
1995: Did not qualify
1999: Pool

One to Watch
David "Hakkies" Husselman (scrum-half)

David Husselman is the key man in the Welwitschias team and a vital link between backs and forwards. He is a lively, decisive player able to organize his pack and generally dictate play. Husselman was brilliant for the Mpumulanga Pumas in the 2002 Currie Cup in South Africa and a key player for the Cats in their last five Super 12 campaigns. Born in Tsumeb, he made his debut for Namibia against Arabian Gulf in Nairobi in a World Cup qualifying game but missed his country's appearance in the 1999 finals through injury.

Romania

For the third tournament in succession, **Romania** find themselves in the same pool as Australia. With Argentina and Ireland also lined up against them, it's going to be a brutally hard campaign for the Romanians.

Romanian rugby during the 1970s and early 1980s was as strong as anywhere in Europe and had there been a World Cup in 1983 there is every possibility that they would have reached the semi-finals. Under the Ceaucescu regime, the sport was afforded great importance among the services and police.

The overthrow of Ceascescu – during which former Romanian captain Florica Murariu, was killed – and the economic collapse of the country threw Romanian rugby into a spiral of despair, which hit rock-bottom in November 2001 in a 134–0 defeat against England at Twickenham.

From that low point they have begun the long haul back. Bernard Charryerre, a successful former France U19 coach, was given leave of absence from the French Federation to take over as coach until the World Cup. His passion and organizational skills were soon seen as Romania bounced back to win the European Nations Cup just four months later.

The players

Under their new coach, Romania have tried to expand their old-fashioned forward-orientated game which has brought out the best in players like centre Romeo Gontineac and fly-half Ionut Tofan. Wing Mihai Vioreanu is another to have emerged, while up front a new breed is replacing the old.

Flanker Alexandru Manta, currently with Begles-Bordeaux, is a dashing, aggressive openside, while Ovidiu Tonita is a fine prospect at lock and has already broken into the Biarritz side. Nicolae-Dragos Dima is learning his trade as a prop at Toulouse, while hooker Marius Tincu is doing likewise at Pau and prop Sorin Socol at Brive.

Qualification for Australia was secured impressively when they thrashed Spain 67–6 at Iasi, while earlier they had given a good account of themselves in Palma, before losing 25–17 to Italy.

Romania's World Cup history

The Romanians have participated in the final stages of all four previous World Cups, bagging a win for themselves every time except in 1995 when they produced one of their best-ever performances before losing 21–8 to eventual winners South Africa. In 1987 they defeated Zimbabwe 21–20 at Eden Park; in 1991 they celebrated a 17–15 triumph over Fiji at Brive and last time out they won a classic encounter against the USA at Lansdowne Road 27–25.

One to Watch
Petre Mitu (scrum-half)

A tough lively player who was outstanding in the 1999 World Cup, Mitu began his playing career as a full-back with the Gloria Bucharest club, making his international debut against Poland in 1996 as a full-back aged 19. He was appointed to the Romanian captaincy soon after the 1999 World Cup but both his 2001 and 2002 seasons were badly disrupted by knee injuries, though he was approaching his old form at the end of last season. He is now playing top-class French First Division rugby every week with Grenoble, having moved from second division Aurillac.

Team Name
The Oaks

Playing Strip
Yellow jerseys with blue trim, blue shorts

Website
www.rugby.ro

World Cup Record
1987: Pool
1991: Pool
1995: Pool
1999: Pool

Rugby World Cup **1987**
David Kirk

The 1987 World Cup was something of a shot in the dark. Nobody quite knew if it would take off and become world rugby's premier tournament or if it would be an expensive non-event. England, for example, were unsure for a long time whether to accept the invitation to compete. Eventually it all came together and it fell on young David Edward Kirk to hold the Webb Ellis Trophy aloft for the first time.

Kirk, a product of Wanganui Collegiate and Otago University, where he studied medicine, played international rugby for just four years. He had another life to lead, but he hung around just long enough in the game to claim the ultimate crown.

Fast, elusive, tough, nimble – Kirk had all the attributes to be a world-beater but

initially struggled to nail down a place in the All Blacks team as the world-class Dave Loveridge gave New Zealand other options at scrum-half until injury reduced his effectiveness.

By 1986 Kirk was well established and had been selected for the tour of South Africa when politics intervened and the trip was cancelled. An unofficial Cavaliers tour was organized but both he and wing John Kirwan withdrew. Kirk was still in the ascendancy though and later captained a New Zealand Barbarians squad on a short tour of Britain that had the hallmark of a run-out for the Blacks' potential World Cup team.

Eventually, in the summer of 1987, the inaugural World Cup was about to start when, just two days before the opening game, the All Blacks captain, Andy Dalton, was struck down with a serious hamstring injury. The effect was twofold. A young Sean Fitzpatrick was brought in at hooker,

a position he occupied for the next ten years, and Kirk was asked to captain the side.

Kirk was a natural leader and diplomat and guided his team effortlessly through the pool stages and knock-out rounds. They encountered some resistance from Scotland in the quarter-finals but swept past Wales in the semi-finals and were simply too good for France in the final, which they won 29–9, Kirk scoring one of their tries with a typical forceful dash.

An historic moment

In the chaotic scenes afterwards Kirk was eventually called forward to receive the trophy – a moment of history, incredibly, captured by just one photographer who had been nominated by the photographers pool to be allowed into the Grandstand. This was Russell Cheyne, who was then working for Allsport.

Kirk's tired, blood-spattered but happy

Left: **A job well done. David Kirk lifts the inaugural World Cup for New Zealand.**
Above: **Kirk scoring the second of New Zealand's three tries against France.**

image was wired around the world and a tournament was born. The man himself, however, was nearly done with international rugby. After captaining New Zealand to a Bledisloe Cup victory over Australia the following month – his last ever Test – he packed his bags and flew to England to take up a two-year Rhodes Fellowship at Oxford University, which he had already delayed a year to make himself available for the World Cup.

While at Oxford he won two Blues – one win, one loss – and, after completing his studies, returned to New Zealand to work as a policy advisor in the Prime Minister's office. He also contributes regularly as a journalist on rugby affairs across the world.

France

No matter what the competition, you should never discount the **French**. Possibly the most gifted natural rugby players on earth, the World Cup has thus far eluded them, but on the hard ground surfaces in Australia it takes no great leap of imagination to see them returning home with the Webb Ellis Trophy.

Fabien Galthie quickly gathers and clears the ball.

Bernard Laporte's team weren't quite at their best in the Six Nations, though it should be noted that even in defeat they outscored England by three tries to one at Twickenham. After that, the steam went out of France's season and defeat by Ireland at Lansdowne Road saw them at their complacent worst. In truth, eyes were already turning to Australia because there was nothing left in the Six Nations for France.

The players

France are a team of all the talents, starting at full-back where Clement Poitrenaud is just about repelling all-comers for his No. 15 shirt – notably Nicolas Brusque of Biarritz and Nicolas Jean-Jean from Toulouse. On the wings, Aurilien Rougerie and Toulouse's speedster Vincent Clerc are the likely starters, though David Bory and Christophe Dominici remain in the frame.

At centre, the powerful Damien Traille has built on his promising start in 2002 and confirmed his importance to the team, for his unstoppable bursts and his siege-gun kicking, and those trademark long-range attempts at goal.

Thomas Castaignède, the artful dodger

of French rugby, has made a heartening return from two years of injury misery, and looked back to his best against Wales in their final Six Nations game, but Laporte faces a real dilemma here. There is no doubt that collectively the French back division were twice as effective in 2002 when Tony Marsh – born and raised in New Zealand but a long-time resident of Montferrand – was there to cement things together. Marsh has been undergoing chemotherapy treatment but, if he can recover, is a must selection.

Strangely, in a side so brimful of creative talent, fly-half is problem position for Laporte. Ideally he would want the solid, conventional skills of Merceron but his form dipped after the

Team Name
Tricolores

Playing Strip
Royal blue jerseys with red piping, white shorts

Website
www.ffr.fr

World Cup Record
1987: Finalists
1991: Quarter-finalists
1995: Semi-finalists
1999: Finalists

Ruck and Maul

The V-sign insult was invented to show the French that English archers still retained their bow fingers. The French used to chop off prisoners' bow fingers.

Song

"La Marseillaise" (national anthem)

Half-time Tipple

Kronenbourg
The light, delicate Kronenbourg beer has a respectable pedigree dating back to the seventeenth century. After a glass or two, *ça ne fait rien!*

One to Watch

Olivier Magne (flanker)

Since emerging from France's Sevens side at the start of the 1997 season, Montferrand flanker Olivier Magne has blazed a trail across the rugby world with his aggression and ball skills allied to the pace and stamina of a potential Olympic 400m champion. He is an exceptional player who is always seen to best effect when France are in an expansive mood. A key member of three Grand Slam winning teams, his command performance against Josh Kronfeld in the 1999 semi-final at Twickenham was arguably the great individual display seen in the World Cup. If France are to win in Australia, they will need Magne at his very best.

2002 Grand Slam and the French coach has therefore been experimenting. The talented François Gelez is one possibility though he can be a little erratic, while the multi-talented Frederic Michalak is another very strong contender – the Toulouse man has to be included somewhere. Castaignède is available at No. 10 if required. Anybody who saw him give one of the finest-ever displays from an international fly-half, in 1997 when France blitzed Wales 51–0, will marvel at Laporte's breadth of choice.

At scrum-half, all France will be hoping that Fabien Galthie's increasingly fragile body can hold up just a little longer – the master tactician from Stade Français is vital to their effort – though Laporte will have been encouraged by the thoroughly competent and confident displays of Dimitri Yachvilli in his absence.

Up front, France will be relying largely on experience. The back five has selected itself in recent seasons. Olivier Brouzet and Fabien Pelous are the most experienced international second-row combination in world rugby and would love to finish their careers in a blaze of glory, while the back row of Olivier Magne, Serge Betsen

and the powerful young Basque, Imanol Harinordoquy, has few equals.

Betsen was the subject of a few well-chosen words from Laporte after conceding too many penalties against Ireland in Dublin and Imanol wasn't quite so dynamic as in the previous Six Nations, but that was all a direct result of France generally not firing on all cylinders. If the entire French fifteen are right mentally, their back row will deliver.

Former captain Raphael Ibanez, who led his side to the 1999 finals, seems to be defying the years as well as those who wrote his rugby obituary, and he remains the first-choice hooker while Jean-Jacques Crenca has established himself at loose head. What remains to be seen now is whether Pieter de Villiers is forgiven after testing positive for cocaine and can be reinstated in the front row at tight head. De Villiers is a formidable player, whose top of the ground athleticism is well suited to Australian conditions, and he has been badly missed.

France's World Cup history

Despite never winning the trophy, France have a proud record in the World Cup. Twice they have fought their way memorably through to the final, losing to New Zealand in 1987 and Australia in 1999. In 1995 they lost narrowly to South Africa at the semi-final stage in the rain of Durban and only in 1991 did they really disappoint, ironically when they enjoyed home advantage at the Parc des Princes in Paris. They were outgunned and outfought that day, going down 19–10, and the memory still hurts, especially for Galthie who was his side's youthful scrum-half that day.

Scotland

Scotland's World Cup campaign will represent the coaching swansong of Ian McGeechan, so look out for an extra-special effort from the man himself and the players he commands.

McGeechan – who coached the Lions in Australia, New Zealand and South Africa and guided Scotland to the 1990 Grand Slam – will be pitting his wits against the world's best sides for the last time and will have been working feverishly behind the scenes in anticipation of the challenge for the last 18 months.

A mixed Six Nations underlined the need to construct a ball-winning pack and to increase their options behind the scrum. Scotland have also got to rediscover the art of playing for 80 minutes – they have become very patchy, capable of excellent periods of sustained pressure but then losing concentration and conceding soft scores.

The players

McGeechan has to accentuate the positive. Glenn Metcalfe is a fine attacking full-back but is too rarely given the space to operate in. Chris Paterson is a classy performer blessed with pace and imagination but he can look an isolated figure on the wing – he needs to be involved more. The same can be said of Kenny Logan, a veteran these days but playing some of his best attacking rugby in years.

In the absence of world-class talent at centre, Scotland must be pragmatic and use what they have to best effect. Jamie McLaren is as strong as a horse and not afraid of hard work, while Andy Craig is promising and has deceptive pace. Gregor Townsend – and surely McGeechan will give Townsend his head at fly-half – must

Scotland's Chris Paterson battles it out with Tony Marsh.

somehow bring these disparate talents into play. A lot of pressure will rest on his shoulders; he is the key if Scotland are to kick on.

Townsend can at least rest assured that any possession secured by his pack will be quickly and efficiently distributed by Bryan Redpath, who was probably the pick of the scrum-halves in the Six Nations. Redpath is brave and quick around the base and if anything should sometimes take a little more on himself. He is also an inspiring

Team Name
Scotland

Playing Strip
Navy blue jerseys, white shorts

Website
www.sru.org.uk

World Cup Record
1987: Quarter-finalists
1991: 4th
1995: Quarter-finalists
1999: Quarter-finalists

leader who never lets his country down.

Up front Scotland must rediscover the form that saw them take South Africa apart last November. Simon Taylor is a world-class operator at No. 8, one of the quickest forwards in world rugby, and must be used, ball in hand, whenever possible. The remaining Scotland forwards have got to find ways of supporting their man; too often Taylor outstrips his colleagues and becomes isolated. That's not his fault, it's theirs. Andy Mower was handed the unenviable task of trying to replace Budge Pountney and is learning all the time, while Martin Leslie and Jason White will compete for the blindside spot.

Scot Murray – still a brilliant line-out operator, though he needs to contribute more around the park – and Nathan Hines look like a handy second-row partnership and in the front row Scotland have got to dig in and fight. Gordon Bulloch is

a class act at hooker, Bryan Douglas has developed well and Tom Smith remains in situ, a superb operator in the loose who must first, however, pay full attention to his duties in the tight.

Scotland's World Cup history

No matter what the state of Scottish rugby, they have generally risen to the occasion in the World Cup and, at the very least, performed to the outer limits of their capabilities and sometimes beyond. In 1987, after qualifying impressively for the quarter-finals, they had the misfortune to meet eventual winners New Zealand. Although they lost 30–3, the Scots restricted the rampant All Blacks to just two tries and the Kiwis were definitely flattered by the score-line.

Four years later should probably have been their moment as their superb Grand Slam side of 1990 went into action. Everything went smoothly up to the semi-finals but then, with the auld enemy England at home, they lost the tightest of games 9–6, with Gavin Hastings of all people missing one simple kick in front of the posts.

One to Watch

Bryan Redpath (scrum-half)

Redpath is an extremely tough character at scrum-half who never shirks the physical demands of top international rugby. Small and agile, he fires out a superb service for his fly-half and, over the years, Scotland have generally played their best rugby when he has been working in tandem with Gregor Townsend at fly-half. He lived in the shadow of Gary Armstrong for a while but added polish to his game during a spell with Narbonne in France and has been absolutely superb for Sale over the last two seasons. He is a captain who leads by example. Scotland will be relying heavily on Redpath for inspiration.

Ruck and Maul

Haggis hurling has become an international sport, with events in Australia, New Zealand and North America.

Song
"Flower of Scotland"

Half-time Tipple

Caledonian 80/-
Brewed in Caledonia's original Victorian brewhouse, the 80/- has a rounded and distinctive flavour. Could provide that Grand Slam!

Onwards to South Africa and, in the view of many, this was Scotland's best World Cup side but not a team blessed with luck. In the pool stage they were all set for a famous win over France in Pretoria and a relatively simple quarter-final against a struggling Ireland, when Emile Ntamack stole in for a try and condemned them to a match against the invincible-looking All Blacks. Even then the Scots blazed away bravely in Gavin Hastings' last international before losing a memorable game 48–30.

Finally, four years ago they again reached the quarter-finals and, although there was never much likelihood of them defeating the All Blacks, they performed better than expected. The Scots are always up for the Cup and need watching in Australia.

Fiji

Fiji remain the great enigma of world rugby. Along with the French, they are the most gifted and natural runners and passers in the game and it is no surprise that they traditionally develop such outstanding Sevens players.

Sisa Koyamaibole pursues Scotland's Simon Taylor during an international friendly match.

should not be unduly worried about their pool opponents. All are beatable on their day and, when it comes to Scotland, one of Fiji's greatest-ever days came in 1998 when they thrashed the touring Scots.

The players

Potentially Fiji's back division is breathtaking. Full-back Alfred Uluinayau was a sensation in the 1999 World Cup and has been playing in Japan ever since, while Southland's Norman Ligairi is another attack-minded full-back.

On the wing Fiji can select from four of the most devastating runners in the game – Northland's Fero Lasagavibau, Marika Vunibaka from Canterbury, Vilimoni Delasau from Stade Montois in France and the much sought-after Rupeni Caucau, a star of this season's Super 12 and a member of the Fijian squad that took a silver medal in the Commonwealth Games Sevens. So

They also produce hugely strong, very physical forwards but to date have never quite worked out how to transfer that power into a world-class competitive pack. The problem, essentially, is that everybody enjoys the running and handling so much that the basics of scrummaging, line-out lifting, mauling, rucking and scrapping on the deck for possession sometimes seem a chore.

The hard grounds of Australia should suit them and they'll definitely enjoy the heat of Brisbane and Townsville up in Queensland. And, the French apart, they

Team Name
Fiji

Playing Strip
White jerseys, black shorts

Website
www.teivovo.com

World Cup Record
1987: Quarter-finalists
1991: Pool
1995: Did not qualify
1999: Quarter-final play-off

Ruck and Maul

In days gone by, Fiji was known as the Cannibal Isles.

Song
"Meda Dau Doka"
(national anthem)

Half-time Tipple
Kava
The crushed roots of the kava plant, native to Polynesia, make an intoxicating drink. Do wear a skull cap when sipping this one!

impressive has been Caucau, there have allegedly been moves from the New Zealand Union to get him to switch to the All Blacks – not the first time the Kiwis have tried to poach outstanding talent from the Pacific Islands. Whether the exotically talented but inconsistent Waisale Serevi will be directing operations from fly-half remains to be seen. It could be that the safer, steadier Nicky Little is chosen to partner Jacob Rauluni at half-back.

One to Watch
Vilame Satala (centre)

The huge, long-striding centre comes from a big rugby-playing family and could re-emerge from a dip in form to play a major role again in the World Cup. As you would expect, he is a product from Fiji's successful World Cup and Commonwealth Games Sevens squads and he moved forward into the 15-man game to make a big impact in the 1999 World Cup when he was included in many critics' team of the tournament. Since then, he has enjoyed a spell with Mont de Marsan in France, alongside Serevi, and most recently at Harlequins where he has struggled, to date, to make the impression expected of him. His reputation is on the line so expect some big performances.

Up front, coach Mac McCallion, a former New Zealand Maori captain, has really got to start cracking the whip. Lock and captain Simon Raiwalui and hooker Greg Smith are seasoned performers, as is flanker Seta Tawake. The big hope is that Sisa Koyamaibole, currently playing for Toyota in Japan, comes through as expected. The massive 20-stone No. 8 is a fearsome sight on the charge and is also a Fiji judo player. Put the strength and aggression together and potentially you have a world-beater.

Fiji's World Cup history
The Fijians have their own pre-match war dance, similar to the All Blacks' "haka", called the "cibi", which begins, "Ai tei vovo, tei vovo" ("Make ready, make ready!"), while on their shirts is a coconut palm. Spectators have been known to scale palm trees to get a cheap view of the rugby and boys sometimes stuff roundish objects with coconut leaf and beard to form a makeshift rugby ball.

Religion also plays a key role in Fijian rugby, as it does in their way of life. Many of the squad are devout Christians and are quietly very proud of their faith. Prayer sessions are as important as training sessions when the team is on tour. The strength of their faith was demonstrated at the 1997 Rugby World Cup Sevens tournament where the team jersey was emblazoned with the words "Philippians 4:13", a reference to a Bible passage which reads: "I can do all things through Him who strengthens me."

The local provincial tournament, known as the Telcom Cup, is keenly contested by the 34 provincial unions and provides a focus for rugby at home. Rugby remains the chosen sport for young men in Fiji, with the 600 clubs in the country boasting 25,000 junior players guided by 1,200 accredited coaches. There are 30,130 registered senior players and 200 trained referees to officiate in their regular matches.

There have been some great Fijian players, including Joe Levula, Senivalatai Laulau and current CEO of the Fiji Rugby Union, Pio Bosco Tikoisuva. This small country has also provided many top players for other countries. Winger Joeli Vidiri, who played for New Zealand, the great All Black centre Walter Little and Wallaby flanker Ilie Tabua all hail from Fiji.

In 1987 Fiji made the quarter-final of the Rugby World Cup and, but for a couple of cruel bounces, could have beaten France, the eventual losing finalists. In 1999 they again looked set to cause a huge upset against France, but when a highly controversial penalty try was awarded against them, things went awry. They did make the quarter-final play-off, but lost 45–24 to England at Twickenham.

Japan

Under young coach, Shogo Mukai, a former Japan full-back who enjoyed conspicuous success coaching Toshiba, Japan are beginning to build their best team in years.

They are captained by Takuro Miuchi, a tough, no-nonsense flanker with considerable physical presence, who took over last summer and fired the team with his own determination and ambition. He slots into a back row which is rated as the best ever produced by Japan, with powerhouse Yuya Saito, a powerful tackle-breaker at No. 8 and the canny, hard-nosed Naoya Okubo at blindside flanker.

The pack has been strengthened recently by the emergence of a potentially world-class prop in Ryo Yamamura who was destined for a life as a professional sumo wrestler before he discovered rugby.

Another to watch out for is lightning wing Daisuke Ohata, who scored eight tries in Japan's astonishing 155–3 win over Chinese Taipei in a World Cup qualifier last year. Other top players are young full-back Hirotoki Onozowa, experienced centre Yukio Moroki and former New Zealander Andy Miller who pulls the strings at fly-half. Miller has lived in Japan for five years, has become a Japanese national and now speaks the language fluently. Other imported players are flankers Dean Anglesey, lock Adam Parker and centre Reuben Parkinson.

Grassroots rugby

The elite rugby is played by the top company teams – Kobe Steel, NEC, Suntory, Toshiba and Sanyo, who put top dollars and extensive resources into trying to trump their business competitors on the playing fields. Rugby is also very popular at universities. With 48 affiliated provinces, a surprisingly large number of 4,785 clubs boasting over 80,000 senior players, rugby at the grassroots in Japan is buoyant.

The Japanese are proud to have qualified and competed in all four World Cups to date but are also embarrassed by their poor return – just one win, though that was a thumping 52–8 win over Zimbabwe at Ravenhill back in 1991. The Japanese recoil at the horror, however, of their infamous 145–17 thrashing at the hands of New Zealand at Bloemfontein in 1995 and are determined to set the record straight. Opponents who relax this time round might get a rude surprise.

Team Name	
Cherry Blossoms	●

Playing Strip
Red-and-white hooped jersey, white shorts

Website
www.rugby-japan.or.jp

World Cup Record
1987: Pool
1991: Pool
1995: Pool
1999: Pool

One to Watch
Daisuke Ohata (wing)

Ohata is an extraordinary bundle of energy and power, who burst on to the scene at the Hong Kong Sevens when he was voted player of the tournament. Already his country's leading international try-scorer, Ohata is also famous for regularly winning the nation's Kin-niku Banzuke TV programme, which is essentially Japan's own unique version of the BBC's Superstars. Top competitors from every sport are pitted against each other in strength and stamina tests and Ohata invariably leaves all-comers trailing.

USA

Often labelled the sleeping giant of world rugby, the United States have yet to achieve lift-off, but if ever they do rugby's world order will quickly change. Here's why America might just be the team of the future

The big problem with rugby in the USA is that the game is considered almost exclusively a social sport, light relief from American football, ice-hockey, basketball and baseball, which are played only at elite level. There are plenty of rugby players in the USA, possibly 50,000 or more, but they are predominantly playing for fun.

The players

The team has some impressive material, though, and could yet cause problems if taken lightly. Dan Lyle is a world-class operator at No. 8, while Dave Hodges, a stalwart with Llanelli in recent seasons, is another all-round talent in the back row.

Luke Gross, once with Harlequins and now with Llanelli, is another powerhouse in the second row, packing down alongside Alec Parker, and look out for rapidly developing 20-stone prop Mike MacDonald. Another who might make the grade is Jacob Waasdorp, a 20-stone-plus prop.

In the backs, scrum-half Kevin Dalzell is a clever player , while his likely half-back partner is Mike Hercus. Former South Africa Sevens representative Riaan Van Zyl has made a big impression and former England A cap Jason Keyter can be a clever and elusive runner. Full-back Link Wilfley has a powerful boot, young centre Kain Cross is developing quickly and centre Philip Eloff is another with a South African background.

USA's World Cup history

The Eagles' only World Cup victory was in 1987, when they defeated Japan 21–18 in Australia, losing their other two matches to England (34–60) and Australia (47–12). They drew another tough group four years later when they went down 46–6 to New Zealand, 37–9 to England and, worst of all, 30–9 to Italy at Otley.

In 1999 they found themselves in another tough pool featuring Australia and Ireland. After losing to Ireland 58–8, they slipped to a 27–25 loss against Romania in a fine game. They finished with a 55–19 defeat in Limerick, a game notable for the only try scored against the Wallabies in the 1999 tournament. This time around, qualification was through the back door, the USA having under-performed in the increasingly tough American pool, finishing only third behind Canada and Uruguay. The Eagles recovered quickly and hammered Spain in the two-legged repechage tie.

Team Name
Eagles

Playing Strip
Red and white

Website
www.Usa-eagles.org

World Cup Record
1987: Pool
1991: Pool
1995: Did not qualify
1999: Pool

One to Watch
Dan Lyle (No. 8)

Dan Lyle was heading for a military career, like his father, before he decided to pursue his rugby dream. He is a superb all-round athlete and sportsman who is also highly proficient at basketball and American Football and those skills can be seen to good effect on the rugby pitch with his deft handling, catching and power play. He first came to prominence on a short Eagles tour of Ireland and subsequently signed with Bath and then captained his country at the 1999 World Cup. He has been plagued with serious shoulder injuries, but when fully fit Lyle is the Eagles' one genuinely world-class player.

Rugby World Cup **1991**
David Campese

Life was never dull with **David Campese** around – indeed the extrovert Aussie wing had lit up the rugby world since announcing his arrival on the world scene in 1982, when he made his Wallaby debut.

There was his outstanding contribution to that marvellous Aussie side of 1984 that won the Grand Slam on their European tour, his consistent excellence in Bledisloe Cup matches against the old enemy New Zealand, and a starring role in Australia's ultimately unsuccessful 1987 World Cup bid.

A fair dinkum Aussie with a dash of Italian flair, he had also become a major attraction at the Hong Kong Sevens and did much to promote that splendid event but, despite everything, he arrived in Britain and Ireland for the 1991 World Cup under something of a cloud.

It all harked back to the 1989 Lions tour of Australia and the final decisive Test in Sydney when his careless, some would say arrogant, pass when retrieving a ball

on his own line gifted a Series-winning try to Ieuan Evans and the Lions. Suddenly, in the public perception, he went from being a joker to a joke. His jibes and banter, which had previously been amusing, now irritated and started getting under people's skin. And we started to examine his game more closely. Yes, he could really play, there was no denying that, but it was his errors and lapses we started to talk and write about.

So Campese was a man on a mission. He had got himself really fit and was trying hard to contain his natural inclination to comment on everybody and everything and wind up the opposition. In Australia's opening game he scored two scorching tries against Argentina at Stradey Park and followed that up with another special in front of a packed Cardiff Arms Park, when

the Aussies thrashed Wales 38–3 in their final pool game.

Next up was that thrilling quarter-final with Ireland in Dublin, Campese scoring another brace of tries as Australia squeezed home 19–18, all of which set the scene for the semi-final against the All Blacks exactly a week later back in Dublin, where the home crowd got fully behind the Wallabies.

Campese's triumph

Campo had the match won for Australia by half-time. First he picked an incredible diagonal line across field to outsprint the entire All Blacks defence and open the scoring in the sixth minute. And then he weaved his way down the right touchline and produced that audacious and incredible over-the-shoulder pass – the

Left: **Catch me if you can! David Campese gathers speed.**
Above: **Campese scores against New Zealand.**

product of all those years playing Sevens – to the supporting Tim Horan, who roared over for a crucial score. There was no way back for New Zealand. The champions were beaten.

Campo hardly saw the ball in the final but he played a decisive role in the build-up, goading England about their boring forward-orientated approach and the need to put on a show for the World Cup Final crowd. Whether it was Campo's verbals or a pre-planned change of tactics we'll never know, but England came out chucking the ball around with gay abandon and proceeded to lose a match and a World Cup they should probably have won.

South Africa

There is always a huge expectation surrounding any **South African** squad and for this one it will be the same. Tournament-winners in 1995 on their debut in the World Cup and placed third in 1999, the Boks have a proud record.

South Africa's Bob Skinstad in action against Wales.

what coach Rudi Straeuli and his management team have been doing this year and it would surprise nobody if South Africa produced something special come the World Cup. England coach Clive Woodward is certainly expecting the real South Africa to pitch up in Perth on October 18 for the most eagerly awaited pool games of the tournament.

In the cold light of day Straeuli, not one to make excuses either as a player or as a coach, will admit that there were at least mitigating circumstances. His squad had been severely weakened by injuries and withdrawals before they even got on the plane and those who did travel were tired and flat. There had also been a rash of retirements among senior players, which took away the hard core of experience within the squad. So that was the explanation. How to rebuild, though?

They have been under pressure ever since their disastrous autumn tour of Europe in 2002 when they slipped to humiliating defeats against France, Scotland and England.

The 52–3 slaughter at Twickenham against England was probably the all-time low point for South Africa; it was certainly their biggest-ever loss. The manner of defeat was also unacceptable, with the Boks reduced to well-publicized outbursts of violence, led by their captain Corne Krige, who completely lost the plot. The Boks seemed unable to match England in any department, something that had never happened to them before.

They went home much chastened, but South Africa is one of the few rugby nations on earth capable of bouncing back from such a massive setback. The country is teeming with powerful committed rugby players – they won the Under-19 World championship in France in April, for example – it's just a matter of identifying and harnessing all that talent and pointing it in the right direction. That's

Team Name
Springboks

Playing Strip
Dark green jerseys with gold collars, white shorts

Website
www.sarugby.net

World Cup Record
1987: Did not compete
1991: Did not compete
1995: Winners
1999: Third

The players

Unbelievably, it was up front that South Africa were taken to the cleaners and that is where Straeuli has concentrated his efforts. First, he has persuaded Andre Venter to come out of retirement and asked Os du Randt to make one final effort to overcome his serious knee injuries. Prop Robbie Kempson has interrupted his spell with Ulster to travel back and challenge again for selection, while Straeuli will be hoping that Bob Skinstad can finally enjoy an injury-free run and begin to maximize his extraordinary talent. Joe van Niekerk is a rapidly developing world-class talent at No. 8 and line-out king Victor Matfield is a world-class operator when fit. They could yet put a mighty pack together.

Behind the scrum there is talent but too often there has been no one to pull it altogether. Although Johannes Conradie has outstanding ability at scrum-half, he has not yet fully stepped into the shoes of Joost van der Westhuizen – indeed the latter has been playing so well again that it is possible he will return for one final World Cup campaign.

Fly-half has been a problem area – some days 'Butch' James looks like the solution, while on others he seems horribly out of his depth. Andre Pretorious and the exciting but inexperienced Brent Russell very much come into the equation. The midfield should be based around Robbie Fleck but the feisty Western Province centre operates on a short fuse, to the detriment of his game. Wider out Breyton Paulse is a player they must bring into the game more often, while to date we have only seen glimpses of Werner Greef's match-winning ability.

The 1995 triumph

What South Africa have to remember is that their famous World-Cup-winning team of 1995 were far from tournament favourites when they set out on their crusade; indeed, they weren't even expected to win their pool, with the then reigning world champions Australia seeded to prevail.

What happened during that extraordinary five-week campaign – aside from a new nation coming together

Ruck and Maul

On sporting occasions, South Africans like to eat ostrich biltong, a wind-dried meat snack, in place of other rugby-playing nations' meat pie and Bovril.

Song
"Nkoso sikelel'I Afrika" (national anthem)

Half-time Tipple
Castle Lager
One of South African Breweries' most popular beers, Castle takes it name from a British-owned brewery founded during the gold rush. A good beer to provide a tight head.

– is that a side grew up together overnight and good players became great internationals. Andre Jubert and van der Westhuizen were always out of the top drawer but suddenly they were joined by du Randt, Mark Andrews, Kobus Weise, Ruben Kruger, Joel Stransky and Chester Williams. South Africa in 2003 have the potential to do that. In pure rugby terms they are at least as talented as the class of 95. What Straeuli has to do is somehow get them in the right frame of mind. If he achieves that, expect the Boks to mount a mighty challenge.

One to Watch
Breyton Paulse (wing)

Western Province wing Breyton Paulse is the joker in the pack for South Africa, the crackerjack wing who can make things happen out of nothing. A happy-go-lucky character, Paulse was brought up in Ceres in the Western Cape, an area famed for its fruit farming, and played for his local farm side before heading for Stellenbosch University. Quick and elusive, Paulse has been a regular try-scorer for the Boks even if they haven't always realized what a talent they have on their hands. Since the retirement of Chester Williams he was worn the mantle lightly of being South Africa's best-known black sports player. Look out for his gymnastic back-flips if he's really happy about one of his tries!

England

Clive Woodward's **England** are pre-tournament favourites, and with good reason. After a storming autumn campaign in 2002 when they defeated New Zealand, South Africa and Australia, they then won the long-awaited Grand Slam in spectacular fashion at Lansdowne Road against the Irish.

England have continued to build and also have memories of a disappointing 1999 campaign to spur them on. If ever an England side are going to win the World Cup and break the southern hemisphere's dominance, you fancy this might be it.

They are a team of many strengths and few weaknesses. Their forward power can be all but overwhelming, while the back come at their opponents from all positions and angles.

The players

Up front Steve Thompson has established himself at hooker, but the competition is fierce in that position, with Jason Leonard, Graham Rowntree, Julian White and Phil Vickery all in the equation, assuming the latter recovers from his back problem.

England's first-choice second row – Martin Johnson and Ben Kay – is as good as any in world rugby and there is strength in depth with Lions Danny Grewcock and Simon Shaw in reserve, along with the likes of Steve Borthwick, Tom Palmer and Chris Jones.

In the back row the old firm of Neil Back, Richard Hill and Lawrence Dallaglio finished the Six Nations together, but they are being pressed mightily hard by Lewis Moody, who had displaced Dallaglio before injury struck, the exciting James Forrester from Gloucester, Joe Worlsey and Alex Sanderson. Whatever combination England put out, they will be selecting from strength.

The massive frame of Martin Johnson always proves effective against any opposition.

Matt Dawson, if fully fit, is the fulcrum at scrum-half and has the ability to raise his game against the bigger opponents. Kyran Bracken and Andy Gomarsall provide excellent back up, but at fly-half the situation is less clear. Before injury struck, Charlie Hodgson was the obvious cover for Jonny Wilkinson but he has been ruled out and Woodward's choice is effectively limited to the experienced Paul Grayson, a terrific goal-kicker but not always the most fluid of links, or Alex King, an inventive attacker but not an international-class goal-kicker. Woodward would love to have Mike Catt back fit and in form.

Team Name
England

Playing Strip
White jerseys, white shorts

Website
www.rfu.com

World Cup Record
1987: Quarter-finalists
1991: Finalists
1995: Semi-finalists
1999: Quarter-finalists

Will Greenwood and Mike Tindall are the established centre pairing with the option perhaps of using James Simpson-Daniel there, while on the wing it is world-class talent all the way with Jason Robinson, Ben Cohen and Dan Luger heading the contenders, though Gloucester's Marcel Garvey is closing rapidly on them all. Josh Lewsey is now clearly established as the first-choice full-back, which has seen Robinson free to create havoc on the wing.

It's hard to locate an Achilles heel when looking at England. The lack of a true replacement for Wilkinson in the case of injury is a possible concern and just occasionally the front row can have an off day, but otherwise it's the best England squad in decades. The Six Nations Grand Slam blew away any hang-ups about their former inability to close out Grand Slams and win big matches away when required.

England's World Cup history

England have always been competitive in the World Cup but ultimately found wanting against the very best. In 1987 they weren't the worst team and qualified comfortably enough for the quarter-finals but then produced their poorest performance in living memory when losing to Wales.

Four years later, it was a case of so near yet so far. The Grand Slam team of that year was a mighty outfit upfront and England muscled their way to the final with an outstanding quarter-final win over France in Paris and then the tightest of victories over Scotland at Murrayfield. All was set for a titanic battle up front against Australia in the final when England, unaccountably, decided to expand their game and started running from everywhere. It was a bold but ultimately flawed approach as they ran out 12–6 losers.

Their 1995 campaign was solid and unspectacular at the pool stage before a memorable victory over the Australians, Rob Andrew clinching the win with a stunning late dropped goal. It all came to an end, however, when they ran into Jonah Lomu and New Zealand in Cape Town.

Four years ago was a curate's egg: middling against New Zealand in the pool (the last time England lost a game at Twickenham), impressive against Italy, Tonga and Fiji and then uninspired and rudderless against South Africa in the quarter-final at the Stade de France in Paris, when Jannie De Beer landed five dropped goals to derail the English chariot. England are much improved since then and will be tougher to beat come the knock-out stages. Many of their senior players could be making swan-song appearances on the big stage and will not want to be denied again.

Ruck and Maul

England has exported the Teletubbies to 113 countries worldwide: that's cultural imperialism with a vengeance.

Songs
"God Save the Queen" (national anthem)
"Swing Low, Sweet Chariot"

Half-time Tipple
Tetley Beer
One of England's top-selling beers, Tetley's has a malty, creamy palate with fine hop flavour. You'll get converted with this one.

One to Watch
Jonny Wilkinson (fly-half)

Still only 24, Wilkinson is international rugby's most reliable goal-kicker but he is so much more than just a points machine. His distribution has become very slick and, pound for pound, his tackling is up there with the very best. Opposition back rows can charge at him all afternoon but they'll never find him wanting. There has been a price to pay, though, with a troublesome shoulder injury niggling Wilkinson for some seasons now. Superb throughout England's Six Nations campaign last season, Wilkinson is a key man in Clive Woodward's squad especially as Charlie Hodgson, the obvious back-up, misses out in Australia with a long-term knee injury.

Samoa

While no one seriously expects either England or South Africa to slip up against **Samoa**, you can rest assured that both the rugby superpowers will be paying the utmost respect to the Pacific islanders who have shown over the last few years that they can never be taken for granted.

Team Name
Manu Samoa

Playing Strip
Blue jerseys, white shorts

Website
www.manusamoa.com.ws

World Cup Record
1987: Did not compete
1991: Quarter-finalists
1995: Quarter-finalists
1999: Quarter-final play-offs

Flanker Semo Sititi launches another counter-attack for Samoa.

Hard, physical, uncompromising, brave, spirited – their commitment is total. Samoa are a remarkable rugby nation. With a population of 176,000, they boast 17,000 regular rugby players – that's nearly 10 per cent of the population and effectively 20 per cent of the male population.

Samoa are coached by the talented John Boe who, as a player, helped Waikato to a Ranfurly Shield over mighty Auckland in 1980, then coached the Province after he retired before switching to the Samoans. A clever, analytical coach, Boe adds a little science and thought to the Samoans' natural aggression.

The players

As ever, securing ball in the tight will be his main concern – you take it for granted that Samoa will have an accomplished back row and backs who can cause damage; it is always in the front five where they have struggled. It is still an area of weakness but at least Trevor Leota, the 20-stone Wasps hooker, has developed into a front forward of international class and the big bonus is the availability of Leo Lafaiali, a Super 12 star with Auckland (and still the only second row to score two tries in successive matches in the Super 12) who has been earning a lucrative living in recent years with Sanyo in Japan.

In the back row captain Semo Sititi, now playing with the Borders in Scotland after a spell with Cardiff, is approaching his prime. The Tuilagi brothers – Alesana and Fereti in the backs, Henry in the back row – are all talented players and young fly-half Fa'atonu Fili is developing nicely with the Marist St Pats club in Wellington and the Hurricanes Super 12 squad.

Wellington's Lome Fa'atau is a class act on the wing and elsewhere the ever-combative Terry Fanolua remains a legend with England's champion club Gloucester, former Sevens star Afato So'oialo remains one of the quickest wings around and the veteran Brian Lima has declared his intention of winning selection for his fourth World Cup. Talking of golden oldies, look out for Inga Tuigamala, still only 33, who although supposedly retired has been registered as a player and is allegedly training – or rather retraining – as a prop if required.

Samoa's World Cup history

Samoa have a proud and remarkable record in the World Cup for a rugby nation with such slender resources, beginning with their extraordinary debut in 1991 when they caught most of the rugby world unawares, although not perhaps the New Zealanders. Two of the all-time great modern-day All Blacks – flanker Michael Jones and wing Inga Tuigamala – were Samoans, while going back another decade or so, that brilliant New Zealand wing Bryan Williams also hailed from Samoa. In Wales, back in 1991, the Samoans were able to make names for themselves playing for their own country – Apollo Perelini, Pat Lam, Too Veaga, Peter Fatialofa, Mattie Keenan and Stephen Bachop became stars overnight.

Their sensational 16–13 win over Wales at Cardiff Arms Park was the shock result of the tournament but their best performance probably came just three days later when they held eventual world champions Australia to 9–3 in the mud and rain at Pontypool Park. They finished their pool with a whopping 35–12 win over Argentina, before the dream finally ended with a 28–6 quarter-final defeat against Scotland at Murrayfield.

Four years later, they were equally tough opponents with Lima, full-back Mike Umaga (elder brother of current All Black Tana Umaga) and flanker Junior Paramore coming to the fore. The Samoans opened up with an impressive 42–18 win over Italy and then defeated Argentina 32–26 before losing 44–22 to England in Durban. The two victories saw them qualify for a quarter-final at Ellis Park where a score-line of 42–14 was flattering to South Africa, who piled on the points at the end.

In 1999 they were back in Wales and opened up with a 43–9 win over Japan at Wrexham before slipping to a 32–16 defeat against Argentina at Llanelli. They now needed to beat Wales at the Millennium Stadium to qualify for the quarter-final play-offs and did so with a magnificent 38–31 win in a vivid display of running and tackling. It was probably Samoa's finest-ever moment

because the Wales they beat that day were an infinitely stronger proposition than the Wales of 1991. Alas, their efforts to reach a third consecutive quarter-final were thwarted at Murrayfield where they lost 35–20 to Scotland.

This time around, they qualified for Australia by finishing second in the Pacific zone behind Fiji after the triangular tournament with the Fijians and Tonga in the summer of 2002. Their games hadn't started well, with a surprise 17–16 home defeat at Apia to Fiji, but picked up drastically with wins in the remaining three games, including a 22–12 triumph in the return game against Fiji in Nadi.

Ruck and Maul

Samoa gave the world the word "tattoo" – it took at least 10 painful days to gain a pe'a, the traditional body decoration.

Song
"Malotuto'atasi o Samoa"
(national anthem)

Half-time Tipple
Yagona Kava
Guaranteed to end up in the "Sin Bin" with his one!

One to Watch
Lome Fa'atau (wing)

Lome Fa'atau has made his home in Wellington, New Zealand, but his family hails from the twin villages of Vailele and Luatuanu'u in Samoa. He only took up rugby six years ago but has quickly emerged as an exceptional talent and was the only Samoa player to earn a Super 12 contract last season. In successive seasons, he emerged as the leading try scorer in the NPC for Taranaki and then Wellington, outscoring the likes of Jonah Lomu, Tana Umaga and Christian Cullen. Like many of the Samoan side, Fa'atau made his mark with the Samoan Seven on the world circuit before making his full international debut against Canada in 2000.

Georgia

Georgia might be rugby minnows in international terms and newcomers to the World Cup but they are one of the most enthusiastic rugby nations on earth and their ancient national game of lelo-burti, dating back over 2000 years, closely resembles rugby.

The Georgians will travel to Australia full of pride for their country. Having split from the old Soviet Union in 1991, they are novices politically, but culturally they have a rich heritage, boasting one of the oldest languages in the world. Being a new state, they really get behind their sports sides. Crowds of 30,000 are not unusual for a home international and can reach 50,000 or more against Russia, the old enemy.

The most successful Georgian club, Aia Kutaissi, won three Soviet titles in a row and twice held the Cup during late 1980s. Then, at the time of 'perestroika' in 1989, the secretary of the Georgian Rugby Union approached the International Rugby Board for recognition of a Georgian Union independent from the USSR and this was granted in February 1992.

The French have also been a massive influence on Georgian rugby – many students return from France with a love of the game. Not surprisingly it is to France that almost all the better Georgian players look to play professionally. Some are good enough to command contracts in the First Division; many others make a living as semi-professionals in the lower leagues.

The players

Guia Labadze is a diamond-tough flanker with Toulon who enjoyed a spell playing semi-professionally in Russia, while Levan Tsabadze, the Montferrand prop, is possibly the side's most accomplished player.

Makho Urjukashvili, who made his international debut as a 17-year-old schoolboy, is a promising wing with Tours who is also developing into a promising goal-kicker. He is joined at Tours by another big powerful back, Tedo Zibzibadze, just 22 but already a veteran of over 20 Tests, while scrum-half Irakli Abusseridze is beginning to win rave reviews with Aurilliac.

Team Name
The Lelos

Playing Strip
Wine, grey and black jerseys, black shorts

Website
www.georgianlelos.com

World Cup Record
1987: Did not compete
1991: Did not compete
1995: Did not compete
1999: Did not qualify

One to Watch
Levan Tsabadze (prop)

Powerful tight-head prop Levan Tsabadze is a former national captain and was recently voted third in an annual national poll for best Georgian sportsman. In his early days his passion was for Greco-Roman wrestling and he claimed a Junior World Championship in the sport before switching to rugby. Born in Rustavi, he moved to France, where he enjoyed spells with Narbonne and Castres, then Montferrand. Unusually for a prop he enjoys Sevens and always shows good handling skills when in possession.

Look out for powerful No. 8 Ilo Zedguinidze, who plays for Rovigo in Italy. A graduate of Tbilisi University in foreign diplomacy as well as rugby player, he is the logical choice to captain the Lelos.

Georgia play rivals Russia.

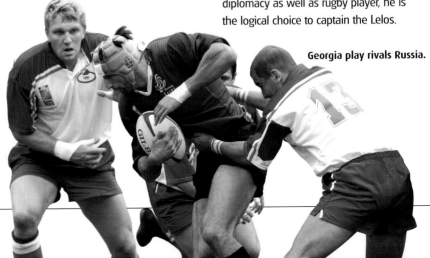

Uruguay

Uruguay may have only 12 clubs and scarcely 1000 senior players of varying abilities to chose from, all of whom are amateur apart from the seven overseas professionals, but they have already proved themselves doughty competitors in World Cup competition.

They can be tough customers. Everyone expected them to be annihilated in 1999 by Scotland and South Africa but they kept the score-lines respectable and still had enough drive left to beat Spain 27–15. Then, in the qualifying pool last summer, they made the worst possible start with three straight losses, but stormed back with victories over Canada, USA and Chile to claim second spot and a place in the finals.

Uruguay's rugby history

Rugby started in Uruguay as an ex-pat sport, being introduced at the Montevideo Cricket Club in the nineteenth century. The sport grew steadily but received a setback in 1930 when Uruguay won the soccer World Cup and football took over. Gradually it clawed back lost ground and the Uruguayan Union was formed in 1951.

The team is currently coached by the best-known figure in Uruguayan rugby, Diego Ormaechea, the granite-like No. 8 who represented his country for 22 years after making his debut at 19 and saying his farewell at the 1999 World Cup. His determination could be seen when Uruguay staged their comeback in the qualifying group last season. Like the majority of his squad, Ormaechea is an amateur: in real life he works as a vet and is a sought-after equine specialist.

The players

Ormaechea has some useful material to work with. Twenty-stone prop Pablo Lemoine made a big impression while playing with Bristol and has also done well since moving to Stade Français. Juan Carlos Bado has served Begles-Bordeaux very well at lock, and the rising star of Uruguayan rugby is the athletic Rodrigo Capo, who has looked equally at home at

lock and at No. 8 playing for Castres.

In the backs, the class acts are captain and centre Diego Aguirre – whose brother Sebastien could well start at fly-half– and Emiliano Caffera from the Champagnat club, who is a promising scrum-half. It's worth keeping an eye out for full-back Juan Ramon Menchaca too – he was the man who kicked four dropped goals in the first half when Uruguay defeated Chile 34–23 in the final pool game.

Team Name
Los Teros (The Bulls)

Playing Strip
Sky blue jerseys, black shorts

Website
www.scrum5.com/uru/

World Cup Record
1987: Did not compete
1991: Did not compete
1995: Did not qualify
1999: Pool

One to Watch

Juan Carlos Bado (lock)

Bado has been playing international rugby for Uruguay for 11 years. At 6ft 5in and a shade over 18 stone, he is a rock-solid member of Uruguay's powerful pack and was ever-present for Los Teros in the 1999 World Cup when they played Scotland, South Africa and Spain. A valuable source of line-out ball, it is in the set-pieces and mauls that his strength really comes to the fore. Born in Montevideo, he is one of seven Uruguayans who have chosen to play professionally overseas.

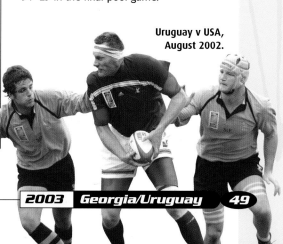

Uruguay v USA, August 2002.

Rugby World Cup **1995**
Nelson Mandela

Anybody who was lucky enough to attend the **1995 World Cup Finals in South Africa** will know that the five-week tournament was much more than a mere rugby competition.

The Rugby simply provided the focus for a new nation – black and white together – as it finally emerged from the dark ages of apartheid. For the host nation it was time to party and proudly proclaim their nationality and the World Cup provided the perfect excuse. Better still, the world and its media were in attendance and could join in the fun.

At the centre of everything was President Nelson Mandela who, during his years of incarceration on Robben Island, had often huddled around the prison radio to cheer on the touring British Lions teams against South Africa. That was then. Now he was the head of a new united nation and it was time to get behind the Boks, the team and institution that above all others had represented white supremacy during the apartheid years.

So Mandela nailed his colours to the mast from the very beginning. He visited the team's training camp in his presidential helicopter as pre-tournament preparations got under way and was in regular contact with manager Morne Du Plessis, coach Kitch Christie and captain François Pienaar, offering support and ensuring there was nothing the team wanted for.

As history records, it was a long, hard

road. There was the pre-tournament hamstring injury to Chester Williams, the face of black rugby in South Africa, there was the massive punch-up against Canada at Port Elizabeth when three got sent off, including hooker James Dalton, who was banned from the rest of the competition, and finally there was the miracle of Durban when the Boks somehow squeezed past France to reach the final.

A tropical storm had swamped Durban and for much of the afternoon it seemed unlikely that the game could be played – in which case France would have advanced because of their better disciplinary record. Referee Derek Bevan eventually took the decision to proceed and South Africa splashed to a 19–16 win, France's Abdelatif Benazzi being stopped half an inch short of the line in the final minute. It was that close.

And so we all trooped off to Ellis Park for the final and South Africa's appointment with destiny. The All Blacks, with the sensational Jonah Lomu seemingly unstoppable, were the strongest of favourites but somehow we knew South Africa would prevail.

A flying start for a new nation

Three moments stand out, two of them directly involving Mandela. The first was the extraordinary fly-over by the South African airways Jumbo jet that buzzed the stadium twice, the second time so low there is a famous picture of a security sharpshooter high on the roof of one stand ducking as the monster screeched over.

The second was at the presentation before kick-off. Up in the press box, we could see President Mandela sitting in the VIP hospitality area and had spotted that he was wearing Pienaar's No. 6 shirt. The roar of approval from the predominantly white South African crowd – all 70,000 of them – as he walked on to the pitch still seems to reverberate years later.

And finally the match was over and the trophy won. Mandela was making the presentations and after he handed over the trophy to Pienaar he couldn't contain himself any longer. He gave the famous double-fisted salute of victory. Somehow everyone knew it wasn't only the World Cup he was celebrating.

Left: **Captain François Pienaar receives the trophy from Nelson Mandela.**
Below: **It's high enough, it's far enough; it's straight enough. Joel Stransky brings home the spoils.**

New Zealand

Anyone who knows anything about New Zealanders and New Zealand rugby will know that the All Blacks will be striving even harder than usual this year to regain that world crown.

Jonah Lomu evades England's Tony Underwood during a 1995 World Cup game.

The humiliation of being stripped of co-host status for the tournament hit hard and even though it was totally down to the administrators, not the players, New Zealand rugby demands some sort of payback on the field.

New Zealand's World Cup history
New Zealand started with a World Cup triumph on their home soil in 1987, but although they have always been a major factor in subsequent competitions, the All Blacks have yet to get their hands back on the Webb Ellis Trophy. That 1987 team was exceptional, with the likes of John Gallagher, John Kirwan, Grant Fox, Dave Kirk, Gary Whetton, Wayne Shelford, Michael Jones and a young Sean Fitzpatrick in full flow. They were virtually unstoppable and to the surprise of no one marched to victory over France in the final.

New Zealand, if anything, were even stronger during the next two years under the leadership of Wayne Shelford, but they made the classic mistake – which England have also made – of peaking between tournaments. By 1991 the Blacks were on a slight downturn. They spluttered through England's pool as winners, were unconvincing quarter-final winners over Canada in the rain of Lille and eventually lost decisively to great rivals Australia in the semi-final in Dublin. A third-place play-off victory over Scotland was little consolation.

Four years later should have been their year. An exciting new team played brilliant rugby and, in the opinion of most critics, were comfortably the best team on view. They did, however, lose the one match that counted – the final against South Africa at Ellis Park.

Under Lawrie Mains, New Zealand had overhauled the team completely, with the exception of Fitzpatrick, an ageless warrior. In came new stars such as Jonah Lomu,

Team Name
All Blacks

Playing Strip
Black jerseys, black shorts

Website
www.nzrugby.com

World Cup Record
1987: Winners
1991: Semi-finalists
1995: Finalists
1999: 4th

Glen Osborne, Marc Ellis, Frank Bunce, Andrew Mehrtens, Justin Marshall and Josh Kronfeld. They played an all-action Barbarians style of rugby that thrilled the crowds but ultimately it didn't bring them the crown.

In 1999, Kronfeld, Lomu, Mehrtens and Marshall, along with experienced lock Ian Jones, were still around but again they fell short, this time running into an inspired France during their Twickenham semi-final. Lomu was again a huge star, taking his total to 15 World Cup tries in two tournaments – a record – but strangely the presence of the great man, when fully fit, occasionally detracts from New Zealand's overall performance. Perhaps they subconsciously rely too much on him in attack. Whatever the case, New Zealand will be looking to attack from all angles this time around.

The players

As the 2003 tournament approaches, New Zealand, as usual, have plenty of international-class players and getting the right selection and mixture is sometimes the main problem. Coach John Mitchell wants his side to be direct, fast and precise up front and to possess a clinical edge behind. Mitchell is a former back row forward and captain of Waikato, who toured with the All Blacks but never gained an international cap. A hard taskmaster, who believes in the old-fashioned virtues, Mitchell cut his coaching teeth with Sale and Wasps in the English Premiership and also served as assistant coach to England, working with Woodward during England's 1999 campaign.

The backs are bristling with talent. At full-back alone are the world-class skills of Christian Cullen, Leon MacDonald and Ben Blair, assuming the latter can recover from injury. Tana Umaga heads a strong cast list at centre, which also includes Aaron Mauger, who has the ability to become a star of RWC 2003. Doug Howlett and Jonah Lomu are the star turns on the wing, although Jonah suffered a recurrence of his kidney problem in the summer and his state of health and fitness is uncertain.

At fly-half they are again queuing up, with Andrew Mehrtens – the first choice in 1995 and 1999 – trying to fight off the challenge of Carlos Spencer and

Ruck and Maul

In the 80s, French agents blew up the Greenpeace vessel "Rainbow Warrior" while it was anchored in Auckland harbour.

Songs

"God Defend New Zealand" (national anthem)
"Haka" (warrior challenge)

Half-time Tipple

Steinlager
The strong hop character of Lion Nathan's Steinlager has made it popular both at home and abroad.
These frosty big boys are just the reward you need after the maul at the bar at half-time.

Tony Brown, while at scrum-half Justin Marshall is trying to do likewise with Byron Kellaher and Steve Devine.

Back row is rarely a problem, with Reuben Thorne expected to captain the side from blindside wing-forward, while tearaway open-side flanker Richie McCaw is the current first choice in a key position for all New Zealand sides. Jerry Collins and Marty Hola are other mighty performers.

Chris Jack and Norm Maxwell are probably the pick of the choices at lock – both are athletic and fast but can sometimes appear lightweight in the close exchanges. Simon Maling is another young second-row forward to keep an eye on. Front row is far from clear-cut but will probably feature Anton Oliver at hooker, with Kees Meeuws and Greg Feek at prop and Carl Hayman and Joe McDonnell also pressing hard.

One to Watch
Doug Howlett (wing)

Former junior sprint champion in New Zealand, Howlett was the star turn during New Zealand's last European tour before the World Cup, scoring brilliant tries against England and Wales when he demonstrated the sort of pace and instinct for a gap that has made him so dangerous in the Super 12s. Another product of New Zealand's successful Sevens squad, he ruffled a few feathers at the beginning of the season by entering into contractual disputes with the Auckland Blues and the All Blacks and threatened to move to Europe, but the issue was soon settled and, barring injury, Howlett is set to become one of the stars of RWC 2003.

Wales

With the exception of a brief renaissance under Graham Henry, **Welsh** rugby has been in decline now for nearly 15 years and a bottom place and whitewash in last season's Six Nations hardly augurs well.

Tom Shanklin ploughing his way through the Italian defence.

Despite everything, however, they do possess talented players – so far seen only in short bursts – with the quality and ability to extend the very best teams.

The draw this time around has been very kind and, although nobody will seriously expect Wales to defeat New Zealand on their home patch, there is no reason why they should not overcome Italy, Tonga and Canada to claim a quarter-final berth.

The players

Wales still have runners and backs to threaten and damage the best. Dwayne Peel and Gareth Cooper have both developed at scrum-half and Welsh fans live in hope that Robert Howley will reconsider his decision to quit the international game. Stephen Jones is the first choice fly-half – always an emotional and key position for a Welsh side – and the likelihood is that Iestyn Harris, now beginning to warm to the Union game, will be used at centre, where Mark Taylor, Tom Shanklin and Jamie Robinson provide options. There is no shortage of choice on the wings either, with big strong runners like Mark Jones, Gareth Thomas and Daffyd James, while the exciting talent of Cardiff's Rhys Williams is likely to be utilized at full-back.

However, Wales have not been producing the forwards of old and badly need a couple of world-class youngsters to come through. Scott Quinnell seems to have retired from international rugby and younger brother Craig has so far not lived up to his massive potential. Pontypridd's Robert Sidoli emerged as a promising lock last season and there were signs that the front row were beginning to become competitive again, with Beb Evans back to something like his best form and Iestyn Harris from Ebbw Vale developing well. In the back row Colin Charvis blew hot and cold but at his best is a world-class player and Wales badly need him firing on all cylinders down under. Michael Owen is a wonderfully skilful No. 8 when in the mood, open-side flanker Martyn Williams was the model of consistency and Llanelli's Daffyd Jones has a big future if he can keep his fiery temper under control.

Team Name
Red Dragons

Playing Strip
Red jerseys, white shorts

Website
www.wru.co.uk

World Cup Record
1987: 3rd
1991: Pool
1995: Pool
1999: Quarter-finalists

Wales' World Cup history

Wales' best showing in the World Cup came in the inaugural year, 1987, when they had just finished a powerful Five Nations season. First up, they defeated Ireland 13–6, a victory they built on with a 29–16 win over Tonga and a 40–9 triumph over Canada. Having qualified for the quarter-finals, Wales then defeated England 16–3 in a niggly, low-quality match in which there were old scores to be settled from that season's Six Nations game. Next came New Zealand in the semi-finals and a humbling 49–6 thrashing – the first major sign of imminent Welsh decline, although some pride was salvaged in the 3rd-4th place play-off in which they defeated Australia 22–21.

Even with home advantage 1991 was a sorry affair, though it is still mystifying why the teams placed third and fourth in 1987 – Wales and Australia – should be grouped together in the pool stages. Anyway, Wales were out of their depth. Not only did they lose 38–3 to Australia, a then record home defeat at the Arms Park, they also lost

16–13 to the virtually unknown Western Samoan team. Wales' solitary victory came in a midweek fixture against a lacklustre Argentina.

By 1995 Welsh rugby was in a sorry state, despite Wales winning the Five Nations the year before. Alex Evans took over as caretaker coach following the sacking of Alan Davies and Geoff Evans was installed as manager. The latter did his team few favours on the day before they met New Zealand when he declared Wales would win because they were "fitter, faster, stronger and better" than the All Blacks. In the event Wales lost 34–9 to the Blacks – it was actually their best performance of the tournament – defeated a woeful Japan 57–10 and then lost 24–23 to Ireland at Ellis Park in a game which decided who advanced to the quarter-finals.

Four years later, again with the boost of home advantage, Wales were much improved under Graham Henry even though they had probably peaked too early and had produced much better rugby in the previous 18 months or so.

Ruck and Maul

Cardiff's new Millennium Stadium was the venue for the 1999 World Cup Final between Australia and France.

Song
"Mae Hen Wlad fy Nhadau" (Land of My Fathers) (national anthem)

Half-time Tipple
Brains SA (Skull Attack)
As its nickname suggests, there's a powerful kick in this malty, fruity ale from brewers Brains of Cardiff. It's a real favourite in the famous City Arms. After a few of these there always seem to be double the number of red shirts on the field.

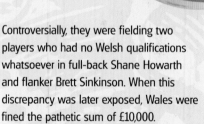

Controversially, they were fielding two players who had no Welsh qualifications whatsoever in full-back Shane Howarth and flanker Brett Sinkinson. When this discrepancy was later exposed, Wales were fined the pathetic sum of £10,000.

Wales opened with a hard-earned 23–18 win over Argentina and stretched their legs mightily to defeat Japan 64–15 but then, for the second time in less than a decade, crashed to a home defeat against Samoa, this time going down 38–31 in what was to the neutral the best and most entertaining game of the tournament. Two wins, however, were enough to see Wales through to the quarter-finals where they performed well against eventual winners Australia before losing 24–9, the score hardly reflecting a tight encounter in which Australia were awarded a ridiculous try at the death.

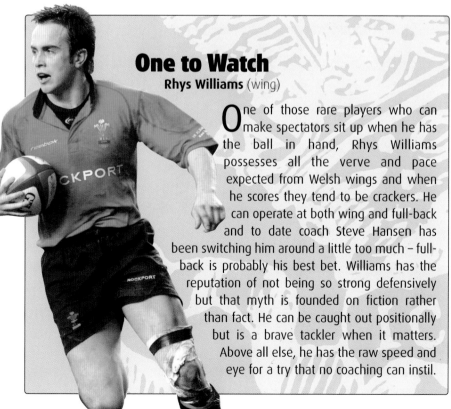

One to Watch
Rhys Williams (wing)

One of those rare players who can make spectators sit up when he has the ball in hand, Rhys Williams possesses all the verve and pace expected from Welsh wings and when he scores they tend to be crackers. He can operate at both wing and full-back and to date coach Steve Hansen has been switching him around a little too much – full-back is probably his best bet. Williams has the reputation of not being so strong defensively but that myth is founded on fiction rather than fact. He can be caught out positionally but is a brave tackler when it matters. Above all else, he has the raw speed and eye for a try that no coaching can instil.

Italy

Despite recording just one win, Italy made great strides forward in the last Six Nations with the improved style of their play and, if coach John Kirwan can work on that, there is every chance of the Azzurri challenging hard for a quarter-final spot.

Gone is the old negative, destructive Italy. Instead they are intent on playing positive, attacking rugby and, when they learn to put that together for 80 minutes, the big scalps will follow.

Kirwan has made a big impact by encouraging Italy to play the rugby they want to play rather than trying to mimic New Zealand or England. As the former All Black wing puts it: "I want Italians to play rugby the way Italians drive their cars – fast, aggressive, close to the edge, a little bit crazy." Kirwan has lived and played rugby in Italy for over a decade and now considers himself more Italian than Kiwi. He speaks the language fluently and understands how Italian rugby players think and react. Sometimes they definitely need the carrot rather than the stick.

The players

Like every side, Kirwan's priority has been to construct a pack and, with the considerable help of fellow All Black Leicester Rutledge, that is exactly what he has done. Front row is rarely a problem: Italy has produced a long line of top props and Andrea Lo Cicero, Giamperio De Carli, Martin Leandro Castrogiovanni and Ramiro Matinez give Kirwan strength in depth.

Team Name
Azzurri

Playing Strip
Blue jerseys, white shorts

Website
www.federugby.it

World Cup Record
1987: Pool
1991: Pool
1995: Pool
1999: Pool

Italy captain Alessandro Troncon takes control against England.

Carlo Festuccia has also emerged as a talented young hooker capable of bringing out the best in his line-out operators.

At lock, Santiago Dellape, Carlo Bezzi, Marco Bortolami and Mark Giacheri are a useful quartet, while in the back row the powerful Andrea De Rossi, the combative Aaron Persico and the aggressive Matt Phillips are the first choice, but they will be pushed hard by Scott Palmer and the youthful Sergio Parisee who made his international debut as a schoolboy against New Zealand in 2002.

Alessandro Troncon is a key man at scrum-half, where he captains the side, but exactly who will partner him there remains unclear. Ramiro Pez, currently playing for Rotherham, is the attacking option with a nose for the try-line, but Kirwan has the option of calling on Diego Dominguez, the second-highest points-scorer in the history of international rugby. Diego is rapidly coming towards the end of his career but Kirwan might still be tempted to call on one of Italian rugby's greatest servants.

The clever darting Giovanni Raineri seems established as first-choice centre but there is a wide choice of possible partners. Cristian Stoice, if fit and properly motivated, is a considerable performer, as

is the immensely promising Walter Pozzebon if he can return fully fit after a miserable 12 months out through injury. There is also a school of thought that, if Mauro Bergamasco is to be used in the backs, his speed and power can be best utilized in midfield. Bergamasco is currently operating on the wing and the deceptively strong and direct Denis Dallan is probably Italy's other first choice. However, Mirco Bergamasco, younger brother of Mauro, is developing superbly at full-back but is equally at home on the wing, while the veteran Paolo Vaccari enjoys playing both full-back and wing and even centre.

Italy's World Cup history

In 1987 Italy had the misfortune to play hosts and eventual winners New Zealand first up and were duly trounced 70–6, Kirwan scoring one of the great all-time tries against the country he was eventually to coach. Considering the demoralizing effect of such a defeat, Italy did well to regain their composure and pushed Argentina hard before losing 25–16 to the Pumas and then finished with a plucky 18–15 win over Fiji.

Four years later, the draw again did them few favours and defeats against

Ruck and Maul

In the region of Liguria, frog risotto, donkey steak and entrail pudding are popular dishes.

Song

"Inno de Merneli" (national anthem)

Half-time Tipple

Peroni Beer

The Peroni brewery produces a number of different styles of beer, perhaps the best-known being Nastro Azzurro. The refreshing, clean taste of this beer can bring out the opera singer in anyone. Don't expect your mates to agree with you, though – they might leave you in the corner!

England and New Zealand were predictable enough, though they battled well against the All Blacks before losing 31–21 at Welford Road, Leicester. Italy's big moment came with a cracking 30–9 win over the USA at Otley.

In 1995 they again managed to grab a win in the pool stages, defeating Argentina 31–25 at East London. They also made England work extremely hard for their 27–20 win in Durban, but were very disappointed to lose 42–18 to the Samoans.

And four years ago they finally lost their record of always coming away from a World Cup with a pool win when they again drew England and New Zealand in their pool. Defeats against those two superpowers were predictable enough but it was a big setback for Italian rugby to lose their third match, to Tonga, 28–25 at Leicester.

One to Watch

Mauro Bergamasco (wing/wing forward)

Exactly where Mauro Bergamasco will appear in the line-up is anybody's guess but the muscle-packed tearaway from Padova is sure to feature prominently in Italy's plans. For the first four years of his international career he operated as a world-class open-side flanker, but then last season coach John Kirwan switched him to the wing, an experiment that seemed set to work until Mauro picked up a nasty thigh injury. If his move into the backs is to be permanent, it could be that his raw aggression and strength may be best utilized at centre. After starting his career with Padova, Mauro moved to Treviso and is keen to experience life in the Premiership after the World Cup.

Canada

Canada's main difficulty lies in gathering the squad from around the world's second-biggest country. They do, however, almost always perform above expectations in the World Cup and they remain one of the toughest sides, physically, you can ever expect to meet.

The Canadian class of 2003 is coached by Australian Dave Clark, who was formerly director of rugby with Queensland and then the Australian Institute of Sport before moving to Canada. Clark brings with him a lot of hi-tech thinking and experience.

The players

Their captain, Al Charron, is one of the great unsung heroes of world rugby, having first starred in this tournament back in 1991 when Canada pushed New Zealand all the way in a dramatic quarter-final at Lille. Advancing years could see Charron appear in the second row alongside Mike James, a world-class lock and top performer for Perpignan and Stade Français. John Tait of Cardiff is another quality international lock.

In the front row Newport's Rod Snow has been a rock for many years, as have fellow prop John Thiel and hooker Pat Dunkley. The live-wire in the back row is invariably open-side Dan Baugh who has struggled with knee injuries in recent years. Ryan Banks is a big hitting blindside or No. 8 and Phil Murphy has got better and better during his spell with Perpignan.

Morgan Williams is a high-quality scrum-half and his brother Jeff, a utility back and a star of the Canadian Seven, is likely to appear in the squad somewhere. Jared Barker is likely to be the first-choice fly-half, though the evergreen Bobby Ross is still pressing hard. Rotherham's Jon Cannon is favourite to take a centre berth, while the leading wings are Winston Stanley, Nik Witkowski and Freddie Asselin.

Canada's World Cup history

In 1987 Canada had a top-class win over Tonga but went down to Ireland and Wales. In 1991 they were superb, defeating Fiji and Romania before narrowly losing to France in Agen and then moving on to Lille for that showdown with the All Blacks. In South Africa, they again defeated Romania and made both Australia and South Africa sweat, while four years ago they thrashed Namibia 72–11, lost narrowly to France and, surprisingly, 38–22 to Fiji, a defeat that cost them a probable quarter-final place.

Team Name
The Canauks

Playing Strip
Red jerseys with black piping, black shorts

Website
www.rugbycanada.ca

World Cup Record
1987: Pool
1991: Quarter-finalists
1995: Pool
1999: Pool

One to Watch
Morgan Williams (scrum-half)

A talented scrum-half who made his mark on the international scene by starring for Canada in the 1999 World Cup, Williams scored two tries against France and one against Namibia. He caught the eye of Begles-Bordeaux, who signed him, and a spell at Stade Français followed. Williams now plays club rugby for Saracens in England. A graduate of the Under 23 Pacific Sport Rugby Academy programme in Canada, he earned his first cap in the Epson Cup in 1999. He then claimed the starting scrum-half position against Wales on Canada's pre-Rugby World Cup tour in August 1999.

Tonga

Tonga is a small nation capable of great things on a rugby pitch if ever they can fully harness all their rugby-playing resources. Players have to look elsewhere to make a living, and inevitably many, like Toutai Kefu and Jonah Lomu, have been poached by Australia and New Zealand.

However, the creation at last of a semi-pro league in the island kingdom has strengthened domestic rugby and if they can get their far-flung stars to return they have the makings of a very useful squad.

Though finishing third to Fiji and Samoa in the Pacific qualifying pool, they romped through the repechage, enabling them to fit in four extra matches and training weeks to their schedule, which is normally sparse. After accounting for Papua New Guinea in the first repechage they hammered Korea 75–0 in Seoul and 119–0 in Nuku'alofa, fly-half Pierre Hola converting all 17 tries.

In all, 11 Tongans scored tries. No. 8, Benhur Kivalu, grabbed four and wing Hola Taniela Tulia and tighthead prop Ephraim Taukafa scored two apiece. The other try-scorers were Sam Hala, Sililo Martens, Nisifolo Naufahu, Inoke Afeaki and Milton Ngaumao, Lisiate Ulufonua and David Palu.

The country and culture
Captain Cook called Tonga the Friendly Islands and the national symbol is a dove. The king is a rugby fan and to help his team prepare for the 1999 Rugby World Cup he bought them a scrumming machine.

Despite a total population of only 100,000 and a playing population of under 800 seniors, Tonga has nonetheless done remarkably well at rugby. It has missed only the 1991 World Cup.

Team Name
Tonga

Playing Strip
Red and white

Website
www.Teivovo.com/pacific-rugby/tonga

World Cup Record
1987: Pool
1991: Did not qualify
1995: Pool
1999: Pool

Tonga's rugby history
Since their first Test in 1924, when they beat Fiji, the greatest moment in Tonga's rugby history came in 1973 when they beat the might of Australia at Ballymore in Brisbane 16–11, scoring four tries to two. Their greatest home victory was over France in 1999. Tonga's World Cup appearances have not been very successful, although they did not come last in their pool in 1995 or 1999. In 1995 the Tongans beat Ivory Coast in a match which is always remembered for the sad paralysing injury to Max Brito, the Ivory Coast wing. In 1999 they battled bravely for an hour or more against the All Blacks and recorded a notable win over Italy.

Like their Polynesian neighbours, the Tongans start their matches with a war dance – the sipi tau – but behind this bold front they are really a friendly people.

One to Watch
Epeli Taione (wing/wing forward)

This exciting player can play top-grade rugby either in the backs or in the forwards, although the likelihood is that he will appear in the World Cup at flanker. Epeli has all the power and strength that you would expect from a Tongan but his speed gives him an extra dimension and, when he's in full flight, probably only his fellow-countryman Jonah Lomu presents a more frightening sight to opposing defenders. He has pursued his professional career with Newcastle in the Zurich Premiership.

Rugby World Cup **1999**
Jannie De Beer

Every player enjoys their 15 minutes of fame, no matter how modest and unheralded, and for South Africa fly-half **Jannie De Beer** that day was the World Cup quarter-final against England at the Stade de France in November 1999.

De Beer, though an accomplished international, was probably a little surprised to be there at all. After the 1995 World Cup Joel Stransky seemed set for a long run in the Boks side but injury cruelly intervened and brought his career to a close. Although De Beer deputized ably when required, it then seemed that Henry Honniball had been chosen to take South Africa forward.

Going into the 1999 World Cup, though, Honniball was injured and De Beer found himself at the helm. The pool stages, however, were disappointing to say the least. The Boks played well enough to defeat Scotland in the one game that really counted but their play was no more than average against both Spain and Uruguay, matches they should have won by massive scores.

They did have an advantage, however, as they settled into their Paris hotel at the start of the week. Because they were pool winners South Africa had a full week to prepare for the big game. England, however, first had to beat Fiji in a quarter-final play-off at Twickenham after finishing second in their pool.

England duly defeated the Pacific Islanders but it was a physical game and it was a bruised and fatigued tour party that climbed on board the Eurostar at Waterloo Station on the Thursday morning less than 54 hours before kick-off. England also had a problem: whether to play Paul Grayson or the young Jonny Wilkinson at fly-half. The question had hung over their entire campaign and had still not been resolved as they arrived in Paris.

Planning and plotting

So while England fretted, South Africa started concentrating early on the big match. In particular Dr Brendan Venter was bringing his formidable rugby brain to bear. Venter was not a happy man, having been sent off and suspended for stamping against Uruguay and then banned. He was desperately trying to find a way of contributing to the South African effort. It was while drinking coffee and watching countless England videos with De Beer, an old friend and colleague from the Free State Provincial side, that he first noticed a chink in the England armour and started plotting with De Beer.

First, England's step-up, Rugby League defensive system organized by Phil Larder was excellent but was a little static and predictable, especially from set-piece scrums and line-outs. Nobody was flying out of the "traps" to put pressure on the opposition fly-half, who was getting a relatively free ride. England were relying on their ability to fan across and contain, especially when Grayson started at

fly-half, as the Boks thought he would against them.

This was very interesting because Venter had a massive respect for De Beer's drop-kicking ability, which he had seen used to good effect for Free State in the rarefied air of Bloemfontein.

"Why don't you drop back another couple of yards in the pocket, Jannie, stand that much deeper, and try a few pots at goal," suggested Venter. "The England defence isn't set up to guard against dropped goals and you could nick some valuable points."

Valuable points! De Beer landed a world-record five dropped goals, every one a beauty, as South Africa marched to a 44–21 win. As one newspaper headline put it, there were "Diamonds in the soles of his shoes"!

Left: **Jannie De Beer lands one of his five dropped goals.**
Below: **And here's another!**

Rugby World Cup
Dream Team

Brendan Gallagher of the **Daily Telegraph** selects his Dream Team to take on all-comers, based purely on the impact star players have made on the four previous World Cups. Australia's John Eales would captain his imaginary side.

15 Gavin Hastings
Scotland
Massively strong and solid full-back who appeared in three World Cups for Scotland. Solid under the high ball, powerful on the surge and a prolific goal-kicker – he is the leading all-time points scorer, with 227.
Other contenders: John Gallagher (New Zealand), Serge Blanco (France), Andre Joubert (South Africa)

14 David Campese
Australia
Brilliant, unpredictable, Aussie wing who played in the first three World Cups, emerging as the star of the tournament in 1991 when his six tries helped Australia to win the title. He scored ten World Cup tries in total.
Other contenders: Rory Underwood (England), John Kirwan (New Zealand)

13 Frank Bunce
Western Samoa and New Zealand
A true ironman in midfield, Bunce was playing for Auckland B in 1991 when he was plucked from obscurity to appear for Western Samoa, the land of his fathers, in the 1991 tournament. Bunce helped Samoa to reach the quarter-finals and four years later was a key figure in the New Zealand team that reached the final.
Other contenders: Jason Little (Australia), Philippe Sella (France)

12 Tim Horan
Australia
Twice a winner with Australia – in 1991 and 1999 – Horan was voted man of the tournament last time round. Very quick, very strong and with an eye for the try-line, he will long be remembered for his score against New Zealand in the 1991 semi-final.
Other contenders: Jeremy Guscott, Will Carling (both England)

11 Jonah Lomu
New Zealand
The all-time leading try-scorer in the World Cup with 15 in just two tournaments, Lomu seems to save his best for the competition. His impact on the 1995 tournament in South Africa was phenomenal: he became rugby's first truly global superstar. He has been fighting a serious kidney complaint since 1996 and his participation in this year's tournament is uncertain.
Other contenders: Chester Williams (South Africa), Jeff Wilson (New Zealand)

10 Joel Stransky
South Africa
Possibly a controversial choice but Stransky comes as part of a half-back package with Joost van der Westhuizen that saw South Africa through to the famous triumph in 1995. The duo did not enjoy the dominance up front of New Zealand in 1987 and Australia in 1991 and had to be more inventive and adaptable. He was as cool as a cucumber and a deadly kicker, but sadly his career was shortened by injury.
Other contenders: Michael Lynagh (Australia), Grant Fox (New Zealand), Rob Andrew (England), Gareth Rees (Canada)

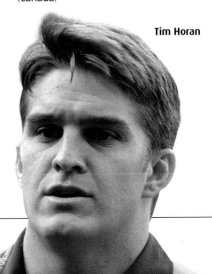

Tim Horan

Joost van der Westhuizen

9 Joost van der Westhuizen
South Africa

Arguably the star man of the 1995 Springboks, van der Westhuizen was an extraordinary player when fully fit, before the knee injuries. Extremely quick, he was also brave as a lion, starting the 1995 final with two broken ribs from the semi-final against France. Don't rule him out of making a comeback for Australia 2003.

Other contenders: Nick Farr-Jones (Australia), David Kirk (New Zealand), George Gregan (Australia), Gary Armstrong (Scotland)

1 Os du Randt
South Africa

Os "the Ox" du Randt was the 20-stone cornerstone of the Springbok pack that delivered the goods in 1995. He was not only a powerful scrummager but also a highly effective all-round forward who showed terrific speed across the ground, before injuries struck.

Other contenders Diego Cash, Matias Coral (both Argentina)

2 Sean Fitzpatrick
New Zealand

A key man for New Zealand throughout the first three World Cups, Fitzpatrick was simply the best and his devotion to the cause set a wonderful example for all around. He was aiming for a fourth appearance in 1999 when a serious knee injury struck.

Other contenders: Brian Moore (England), Phil Kearns (Australia)

3 Jason Leonard
England

The ever-dependable Jason Leonard, who can play both sides of the scrum, has done sterling service for England in 1991, 1995 and again in 1999. Can he make it four in a row?

Other contenders: Olo Brown (New Zealand), Federico Mendez (Argentina), Rod Snow (Canada)

4 John Eales
Australia

Eales, like Little and Horan, is a two-time winner with Australia, captaining them to their last triumph in 1999. A spring-heeled line-out operator and occasional goal-kicker, Eales is probably best remembered for his remarkable try-saving tackle on Rob Andrew in the 1991 final.

Other contenders: Paul Ackford (England), Al Charron (Canada)

5 Ian Jones
New Zealand

Ian Jones just gets the nod to pack down alongside John Eales. A veteran of three campaigns – '91, '95 and '99 – he was one of the most mobile locks in history yet still managed to make a contribution in the tight.

Other contenders: Mark Andrews (South Africa), Martin Johnson (England)

6 Ruben Kruger
South Africa

The tough man of the South African pack from Northern Transvaal, he got through a mountain of work and never took a step backwards. Definitely a man you would want on your side when the going got rough.

Other contenders: Junior Paramore (Samoa), Mike Teague (England), Owen Finnegan (Australia)

7 Michael Jones
New Zealand

In the opinion of many, the finest back-row forward in the game's history, Jones just gets the nod from a host of other all-time greats. There has never been a more threatening flanker in attack than the panther-like Jones and he was as tough as old boots in defence.

Other contenders: Olivier Magne (France), Josh Kronfeld (New Zealand), Peter Winterbottom (England), John Jeffrey (Scotland), Gordon Mackinnon (Canada)

8 Wayne Shelford
New Zealand

"Buck" Shelford never stood for any nonsense up front and with his proud Maori heritage was the heart and soul of New Zealand's magnificent 1987 World-Cup-winning team. He was a rampaging bull of a runner in attack and an immovable object in defence.

Other contenders: Pat Lam (Samoa), Zinzan Brooke (New Zealand), Toutai Kefu (Australia).

Rugby World Cup
History

The Webb Ellis Trophy – named after the student at Rugby School who allegedly picked up the ball during a game of football – is now well established as the world's top rugby event. It is possibly the third-biggest sports gathering in the world, behind football's World Cup and the Olympics – not bad for a tournament that has only existed for 15 years.

The inaugural World Cup was held in 1987 after the Australian Rugby Union, with the support of New Zealand, France and South Africa, had pressed for a World Cup. The ARU felt threatened by the proposed professional rugby union circuit of Australian entrepreneur David Lord.

The British and Irish unions were initially opposed to the idea of a World Cup, so South Africa held the deciding vote. South Africa – ironically, aware it would be unable to play because of the international sports boycott – voted in favour at a meeting of the International Rugby Board in 1985.

1987 World Cup
Sixteen teams gathered in Australia and New Zealand, but there were only three real contenders for the trophy. The semi-final match between the European champions France and favourites Australia is often billed as the match of the tournament. France defeated the Wallabies only to lose to New Zealand in the final 29–9 at Eden Park on June 20.

The gap between the established and the emerging nations was apparent, illustrating that rugby was still far from a global game and that the form of the British and Irish, with the exception of Scotland, was weak. They would claim, with some justification, that unlike the All Blacks and Australia they were strictly adhering to the amateur regulations then in existence.

1991 World Cup
The second World Cup took place in the United Kingdom, Ireland and France, and again 16 nations took part. For this tournament, the IRB invited all member unions to enter qualifying rounds. The eight 1987 quarter-finalists were automatically guaranteed places, while 32 other nations competed for eight other spots. South Africa was still unable to play in the Cup because of the boycott.

England qualified for the final when it beat Scotland in a close match at Murrayfield. The following day Australia secured its final berth when it ended

defending champions New Zealand's hopes 16–6. Australia, who had again entered the tournament as favourites, lived up to expectations this time and defeated England 12–6 in the final at Twickenham.

1995 World Cup
The third World Cup was for many more emotional than either of the first two. It officially proclaimed the return of South Africa to the world rugby stage, and in fact was held in that country. The Springboks proved in the first match of the tournament that they intended to be a force to be reckoned with, when they beat reigning champions Australia 27–18.

Pool play saw some incredible performances but the early stages were marred when the Ivory Coast's Max Brito was paralysed in an accident during a game against Tonga in Rustenburg. The tournament continued and the man who was to become the icon of the 1995 World Cup and rugby union turned out to be New Zealand's youthful, massive left-wing, Jonah Lomu.

In the final, played at Ellis Park in Johannesburg between New Zealand and the hosts, the score was 9–9 after 80 minutes. The match went into extra-time and it was the Springboks' fly-half Joel Stransky who kicked the winning drop goal to make it a 15–12 victory for South Africa.

The emotion did not stop there, as President Nelson Mandela, wearing a copy of the South African captain's No. 6 jersey, presented the trophy. However, the All Blacks continued to allege after the World Cup that they had been poisoned the night before the final.

1999 World Cup

The 1999 World Cup was nominally hosted by Wales but was in practice a re-run of the 1991 tournament with pools in all the four Home Unions and France. This time the competition consisted of 20 teams with the five pool-winners going through to the quarter-finals automatically and the next six best-placed teams competing in three play-off games, a controversial system in which the play-off winners had to play their quarter-finals just three or four days later.

Australia and New Zealand were the most impressive qualifiers, with South Africa seemingly struggling a little in their pool. But it was the Springboks who upped their game against a disappointing England to win their quarter-final game, while Scotland and Wales also crashed out at this stage in the competition. Ireland had already lost their place in the play-offs to Argentina.

An epic semi-final weekend at Twickenham saw Australia sneak home in extra time against South Africa, while in the match of the tournament France recovered from 24–10 to defeat the All Blacks 43–31. Alas, all the French magic was gone at the Millennium Stadium the following week and Australia, whose defence had been superb throughout, ran out comfortable winners.

WORLD CUP RECORDS

BIGGEST WINS

145–17	**New Zealand v Japan** 1995
101–3	**New Zealand v Italy** 1999
101–10	**England v Tonga** 1999
89–0	**Scotland Ivory Coast** 1995
74–13	**New Zealand Fiji** 1987
72–11	**Canada Namibia** 1999
70–6	**New Zealand Italy** 1987
70–12	**France Zimbabwe** 1987

LEADING TRY-SCORERS *

15	**Jonah Lomu** New Zealand
11	**Rory Underwood** England
10	**David Campese** Australia
9	**Gavin Hastings** Scotland
	Jeff Wilson New Zealand
7	**Marc Ellis** New Zealand
	Brian Lima Samoa
	Ivan Tukalo Scotland
	John Kirwan New Zealand
6	**Marcello Cuttitta** Italy
	Jean-Baptiste Lafond France
	Craig Green New Zealand
	John Jeffrey Scotland
5	**Didier Camberabero** France
	Philippe Saint-Andre France
	Glen Osborne New Zealand
	Tim Horan Australia
	Alan Tait Scotland
	Philippe Sella France
	John Gallagher New Zealand

LEADING POINTS-SCORERS *

227	**Gavin Hastings** Scotland
195	**Michael Lynagh** Australia
170	**Grant Fox** New Zealand
163	**Andrew Mehrtens** New Zealand
124	**Thierry Lacroix** France
120	**Gareth Rees** Canada
110	**Matt Burke** Australia
102	**Ganzalo Quesada** Argentina
99	**John Webb** England
98	**Diego Dominguez** Italy

MOST TRIES IN A MATCH

6	**Marc Ellis** (New Zealand) v Japan(1995)
4	**Jonah Lomu** (New Zealand) v England (1995)
	Gavin Hastings (Scotland) v Ivory Coast (1995)
	Chester Williams (South Africa) v Samoa (1995)
	Brian Robinson (Ireland) v Zimbabwe (1991)
	Ieuan Evans (Wales) v Canada (1987)
	Craig Green (New Zealand) v Fiji (1987)
	John Gallagher (New Zealand) v Fiji (1987)
	Keith Wood (Ireland) v USA (1999)

TOP SCORERS

Most points:
126 **Grant Fox** New Zealand (1987)

Most tries:
8 **Jonah Lomu** New Zealand (1999)

Most conversions:
30 **Grant Fox** New Zealand (1987)

Most penalties:
31 **Gonzalo Quesada** Argentina (1999)

MOST DROPPED GOALS *

6	**Jannie De Beer** South Africa
5	**Gareth Rees** Canada
	Rob Andrew England
3	**Andrew Mehrtens** New Zealand
	Joel Stransky South Africa
	Gregor Townsend Scotland
	Jonathon Davies Wales

* per tournament

The awesome Jonah Lomu drags England's Tony Underwood into touch.

Rugby World Cup Quiz

1 Which country is the only one to win the World Cup twice?

2 Who won the last Rugby World Cup for the Deaf?

3 Which side won the Rugby World Cup Sevens in Argentina in 2001?

4 At which venue will Wales play Canada on October 12?

5 Who won the 1999 World Cup?

6 Which French player scored 30 points against Zimbabwe in the 1987 World Cup?

7 By what score did England defeat Holland in a 1998 World Cup qualifier?

8 What is the official title of the World Cup trophy?

9 What is the highest placing Wales has attained in the World Cup? In what year, who did they beat and where?

10 Which player has scored the most tries in a single World Cup match? How many?

11 Who captained New Zealand to victory in 1987?

12 Who scored the very first World Cup try?

13 Who scored the winning try in the 1987 semi-final between Australia and France?

14 Which country did former All Black Frano Botica represent in the 1999 qualifying matches?

15 How many spectators attended the 1999 World Cup?

(a) 1.2 million (b) 1.5 million (c) 1.7 million

16 What points total has Neil Jenkins scored in the World Cup?

(a) 121 (b) 98 (c) 85

17 Which player has scored the most points in total in the World Cup?

18 Who are the only two forwards ever to score four tries in a single match at the World Cup Finals?

19 What is the biggest win by a side at the World Cup Finals?

20 Which Canadian fly-half played in the first four World Cup finals?

21 Who was the top points-scorer in the 1991 World Cup Finals?

22 At which World Cup Finals did Ivory Coast compete?

23 Who scored the only try against Australia's winning team in 1999?

24 Who is the top try-scorer in World Cup history?

25 Who kicked the dropped goal that clinched victory for South Africa in the 1995 Final?

Rugby World Cup Quiz

What's in a name?

Identify the following well-known players in these anagrams:

A A nit saved Jonah (Wales)

B Damp as device (Australia)

C Ace blink (England)

D A frantic boo (New Zealand)

E Please pil Phil (France)

F In vineyard (Scotland)

G Ta chairman yen (South Africa)

H Owe Mel China (Wales)

I Lame Karl (Australia)

J Net is a word (England)

K Bog cleaners (France)

L I change my hall (Australia)

M Fine I'm saved (Wales)

N Hat Joint (Canada)

O Dim Robert (England)

The Ins and Outs of Rugby Tactics

Crash ball

Crash-ball tactics are designed to achieve two aims. Either you want to make contact with the opposition to drag in their defenders, so you can then quickly move the ball wide and take advantage of the space created, or you want to try to burst through the defence at the first attempt and then possibly offload to the quicker men to finish off the job and score a try. No matter the aim, the trick is for the attacking runner to come from deep, at speed, and to pick a line the opposition are not necessarily expecting. Watch how Australia have used Daniel Herbert in past seasons or how Ireland deploy the powerful Kevin Maggs.

Eight-man shove

It's scrum time and you have one objective – to push the opposition off the scrum. You are not concerned with striking for the ball – defending sides rarely try these days – and you don't intend to try wheeling the scrum either. Everybody packs down just that little bit lower and grips a bit tighter as they wait for the shout.

Kicking for the corners

This tactic can come into play under any conditions but especially when you are playing with the advantage of the wind. If you have a good accurate kicker, you work the corners to pin the opposition down in their 22. If you kick to touch in this manner they do admittedly get the throw-in at the line-out, but you can pressurize that line-out to force a mistake or then pressurize

Scotland's Chris Paterson kicking for the corners.

their kicker as he tries to kick the ball back into wind. A good team will encamp in the opposition defence and the points usually come.

Miss pass

This is when you "miss out" one of the back division with a pass, i.e. the fly-half moves the ball directly to the outside centre or the inside centre passes directly to one of the wings or the full-back coming into the line wide out. The object can simply be to move the ball as swiftly as possible to outstandingly quick or powerful runners or it can be to keep the

opposition defence guessing and stretched.

Off the top line-out ball

In defensive situations, when attempting to win your own line-out ball, it always pays to catch, secure and drive the ball before delivering to the scrum-half. In attack, however, you might want the ball as quick as possible, with a favourite ploy being the long ball to the back of your line-out where someone deflects and taps to the scrum-half. England's Lawrence Dallaglio, Scotland's Simon Taylor and Imanol Harinordoquy of France are all past masters of this.

Pick and go

Hard-driving forward play, designed to punch holes in the best-organized of defences. The first player drives forward, low and as far as possible, before going to ground and laying the ball back. The next man in does not allow a ruck to form but simply picks up and goes again. If you can repeat this three or four times, you really will have the opposition defence on the rack as they attempt to backtrack and re-group.

Rolling maul

All the pack remain on their feet and maul the ball forward "rolling" first one way and then the other. Once in motion you have to keep going forward – if you are stopped from making progress, a scrum will be awarded to the defenders. It is a very hard ploy to stop, though, because no one is allowed to drag the ball-carrier down. These tactics can prove devastating from line-outs close to your opponents' try-line. Leicester and England both make a speciality of it, with Neil Back often sneaking over for a try.

Shuffle or drift defence

The old-style rugby union defence, which can still be very effective when you are well organized. As the opposition attack, ball in hand, and start moving the ball wide, you shuffle across and start to hem the attackers in close to the touchline where there is less room to operate. For such a defence to work you have to have faith in the defender inside you; if the opposition cut back, you have to rely on your supporting defenders on the inside to plug the gaps.

Step-up defence

Very much the product of Rugby League coaches coming into the game. Available defenders fan out across the width of the field, just behind the imaginary offside line. As the opposition attacks you step up together to confront them, which should minimize the gaps they can attack.

Wide game

The general term used for those trying to move the ball wide at every possible opportunity. Such a play can work in two ways. If your best and strongest runners are out wide, it could give them a fraction more time and space to work their magic. Alternatively, a team with good ball-handling and continuity skills can keep working the ball "wide" and in so doing begin to tire the opposition defence. Eventually the cracks will appear and you should be able to take full advantage.

Wheeling the scrum

You can do this in either attack or defence. In attack, the purpose of wheeling the scrum in one direction is to take the opposition back row out of the equation, i.e. if you have an attacking scrum and you want to attack the blindside you wheel the scrum towards the openside.

In defence, you have just one object – to wheel the scrum through a full 90 degrees as quickly as possible. If you can achieve that, the law states that the referee has to reset the scrum and you get the put-in. Some refs have a strange idea of what constitutes 90 degrees, but that's the theory any way!

Australia prepare for an eight-man shove against Ireland.

Rugby World Cup
Trivia

World Cup Viewing Figures

1987	**New Zealand and Australia**	300 million in 17 countries
1991	**Five Nations countries**	1.75 billion in 103 countries
1995	**South Africa**	2.65 billion in 124 countries
1999	**Wales and Five Nations countries**	3.0 billion in 140 countries

Aggregate Crowds

1987	**New Zealand and Australia**	600,000
1991	**Five Nations countries**	1,000,000
1995	**South Africa**	1,000,000
1999	**Wales and Five Nations countries**	1,750,000

Gross Profit

1987	**New Zealand and Australia**	£3.3m
1991	**Five Nations countries**	£23.6m
1995	**South Africa**	£30.3m
1999	**Wales and Five Nations countries**	£70m

Net Profit

1987	**New Zealand and Australia**	£1m
1991	**Five Nations countries**	£5m
1995	**South Africa**	£17.6m
1999	**Wales and Five Nations countries**	£47m

Where, when, why and how many? We delve into the facts and figures behind the World Cup.

1 The most tries ever scored by a single player in a World Cup qualifying game is 10, by former Loughborough University student Ashley Billington for Hong Kong against Singapore in 1994.

2 The biggest official crowd in a World Cup match is the 78,000 who watched England play South Africa at the Stade de France in the 1999 quarter-final.

3 Only three players have been members of sides that have twice won the World Cup. All are from Australia – John Eales, Tim Horan and Jason Little.

4 In 1991, brothers Stephen and Graeme Bachop played for separate countries in the World Cup – Stephen for Western Samoa and Graeme for New Zealand. Inga Tuigamala played for the All Blacks in 1991 and Samoa in 1999. Frank Bunce played for Samoa in 1991 and the All Blacks in 1995. Michael Jones played international rugby for Samoa in 1986 but switched to the All Blacks the following year for the inaugural competition.

5 Anybody looking at a picture of the fearsome Jonah Lomu will notice something different about his left eyebrow. Lomu uses a razor to cut the number 11 – his position on the wing – into the eyebrow.

6 Lomu is a massive Hi-fi fan and for a couple of years claimed to own the loudest car sound system in the world. It was so loud that he would often get outside the car and stand about 15 yards away, for safety reasons, before turning it on with his remote control.

7 There was a major behind-the-scenes panic before the World Cup Final in 1995 when it was discovered that Jonah Lomu's Tongan parents did not have New Zealand passports and had, in fact, been living in New Zealand illegally. That of course would have made Jonah, technically, ineligible to play for New Zealand. Needless to say, the necessary paperwork was completed in record time.

Jonah Lomu sporting his "Number 11" eyebrow.

8 There are still those in the New Zealand camp who believe their 1995 campaign was sabotaged when a buffet meal at their Johannesburg hotel on the Thursday before the final resulted in all but a handful of their players being affected by serious food poisoning. Coach Lawrie Mains and the New Zealand management later claimed that a waitress by the name of Suzie had poisoned the food.

9 Russia were eliminated from the 2003 World Cup repechage round against Tunisia for fielding three ineligible players in the previous round against Spain. They were also fined £75,000, though this was later suspended.

10 After the 1999 World Cup Wales were exposed as having played two ineligible players – Shane Howard and Brett Sinkinson – but were fined only £10,000 and warned as to their future conduct.

The greatest comeback ever? France scored 31 unanswered points to seal their semi-final win over New Zealand in 1999.

Ten Great World Cup Tries

1 John Kirwan
New Zealand v Italy
1987

2 Serge Blanco
France v Australia
1987

3 Ivan Francescato
Italy v USA
1991

One of the world's greatest-ever wings, John Kirwan graced the opening game of the inaugural World Cup with possibly his best-ever try, beating eight – or was it nine? – Italian defenders in a sensational 80-yard run as New Zealand set out on their successful campaign. There were obviously no hard feelings – Kirwan settled in Italy, married an Italian and now coaches the national side.

Blanco was a player of extraordinary pace and vision and lit up the rugby world for nearly a decade with his spirit of adventure which seemed to sum up French rugby at its best. It was that spirit which saw France through their epic semi-final against Australia in 1987, with Blanco – bloodied, bowed, but unbeaten – sprinting hard for the corner for their dramatic late winner.

The late Ivan Francescato – he died tragically young in 1998 – was one of four brothers who appeared for Italy. He could play wing and centre but was best at scrum-half. This was his finest moment, sidestepping dramatically three times off his right foot to cut through the Eagles' defence. Fans who watched the match can still see his long black hair swaying with each sidestep.

4 Tim Horan

Australia v New Zealand
1991

Horan was the young centre sensation for the Aussies and read David Campese's mind perfectly as they set off down the right touchline during the Lansdowne Road semi-final against New Zealand in 1991. From nowhere Campese produced his cheeky over the shoulder pass but Horan was on the case, gathered it safely in and powered over for a vital score.

5 David Campese

Australia v New Zealand
1991

This one was all "Campo" as he took it upon himself to beat the Kiwis on his own. With that incredible rugby brain of his, Camp saw that the All Blacks' defence was lying too deep and he picked an astonishing diagonal line across the entire Blacks' back division to score in the corner. So quick was the Aussie wing that the Kiwis couldn't lay a hand on him.

6 Jonah Lomu

New Zealand v England
1995

Could England stop Jonah Lomu? No way. The new rugby phenomenon scored no fewer than four tries against Will Carling's England in their semi-final at Newlands, Cape Town, the first of which left Carling, Rob Andrew and Mike Catt battered and bruised. Had it been a heavyweight boxing contest the fight would have been stopped.

7 Gary Halpin

Ireland v New Zealand
1995

Not a try of great beauty this one, but never has a score given such pleasure to the scorer. The Ireland prop, irritated by tales of Kiwi supremacy all week, powered over from five yards out from a tapped penalty and gave the opposition an outrageous double-handed two-finger salute. The crowd at Ellis Park rose as one man to share his moment of joy.

8 Alfred Uluinayau

Fiji v France
1999

Fiji under Brad Johnston were playing cracking rugby in 1999 and a victory over France would have seen them qualify for the quarter-finals. Alas, a couple of shocking refereeing decisions by Paddy O'Brien eventually deprived them, but not before their full-back electrified the scorching Stade Municipal in Toulouse with a majestic individual try.

9 Jonah Lomu

New Zealand v England
1999

That man Lomu again, and England on the receiving end again. This time it was the pool match at Twickenham and England really fancied their chances. They were doing OK until Lomu got it in space for the first time. Off he went, powering his way past three helpless defenders to score yet another cracker. It was Cape Town all over again.

10 Philippe Bernat-Salles

France v Argentina
1999

France had not impressed in qualifying for the quarter-final but gave notice of their return to form with this magnificent length-of-the-field counter-attack, finished off by Bernat-Salles. It was vintage France and nobody at Lansdowne Road that afternoon would have been surprised at how the French fought their way back against New Zealand a week later.

Above: **Fiji's Alfred Uluinayau dives for the try-line.**
Left: **Ivan Francescato on the way to scoring a dramatic try.**

Semi-final Madness

Semi-finals are always tense and often very exciting and the World Cup has been blessed with more than its share of classics. Here are four of them to cherish and pick the bones over.

1987

Australia 24 France 30

This semi-final is a strong contender for one of the greatest rugby matches ever. Australia were on home ground in Sydney and determined to play in the final against New Zealand. They had a massive pack and fast inventive backs and looked odds-on to do exactly that.

France had qualified for the knock-out stages despite only managing a draw against Scotland and then struggled to overcome Fiji in the quarter-finals, having the advantage of a couple of questionable refereeing decisions.

So the scene was set and the result was an entertaining and dramatic game. David Campese and flanker Dean Codey scored tries for the Aussies, while Michael Lynagh kicked three penalty goals, two conversions and a dropped goal. France, however, matched Australia all the way. Lock Alain Lorieux, enjoying the game of his life, scored a try, as did centre Philippe Sella cutting dramatically off the wing. Patrick Lagisquet, known as the Bayonne Express, also crossed for a score, while fly-half Didier Camberabero converted all three tries and added two penalties.

Going into the final minutes, it was tied at 24–24 as France launched one last, multi-phase attack that nearly broke down on a number of occasions before the ball was finally transferred to Blanco on the left wing who sprinted home in the corner to break Australian hearts. Camberabero added the conversion and France were home and dry.

1991

Scotland 6 England 9

The score-line shows that this wasn't exactly a "try fest" but there's rarely been a tenser, harder-fought World Cup game. There was a lot of "history" to this match,

Mike Teague of England sets up the ball.

largely based on the 1990 Grand Slam encounter, when the Scots had won a famous victory. England were well and truly on their mettle although they started as slight underdogs, with Scotland having won their previous 13 internationals against all opposition at Murrayfield.

Ground improvement work meant the capacity was down to 54,000 and perhaps England didn't feel quite so intimidated as previously. Their side were also more experienced and streetwise than before. They arrived in Edinburgh to outmuscle and stifle the Scots and that's exactly what they did.

Scotland in their turn tried to harry and unsettle the English, and England's back three of Jonathon Webb, Simon Halliday and Rory Underwood had a busy afternoon coping with all the high balls that came their way. Midway through the second half it was 6–6, two penalties apiece for Gavin Hastings and Rob Andrew, when Hastings missed a sitter in front of the posts. It was a key moment. England gradually worked their way back upfield and Andrew secured victory with a short-range dropped goal, the 14th of his international career.

It was a devastated Scotland that trooped off, the last time that those great back-row servants John Jeffrey and Finlay Calder ever represented their country at Murrayfield.

1995

South Africa 19 France 15

It never rains in Durban in June, or so we were constantly told throughout the World Cup, and indeed up until the semi-final weekend it had been largely wall-to-wall sunshine. But come the South Africa–France semi-final at Kings Park and the heavens opened like never before, starting on the Friday evening before the game. An intense tropical depression was sweeping in off the Indian Ocean.

At kick-off time on Saturday afternoon they clearly couldn't play: deep lakes of water were all over the pitch and the rain was still lashing down. Two hours passed. A 20-strong army of black women arrived with brooms and tried in vain to sweep the water aside. Then a couple of helicopters swept low but were only slightly more effective.

It was all getting very tense. If referee Derek Bevan called the game off, under the tournament rules the match would have been awarded to France because they had a better disciplinary record than the Boks. Bevan fretted and frowned. Everyone was getting restless. Eventually he decided to start. Frankly, conditions had not improved one jot and after a brief lull the rain returned more heavily. People talk about the miracle of South Africa's World Cup triumph and defeating the All Blacks. The Boks players will tell you that the true miracle was playing and winning the semi-final.

France, to their eternal credit, did not make a fuss and just got on with the game. Thierry Lacroix kicked five magnificent penalties, the Boks replied with a try by Ruben Kruger and four penalties and a conversion by Joel Stransky. With virtually the last play of the game, France's blindside flanker Abdelatif Benazzi was dragged down half an inch short of the line. The miracle was that close to never happening.

France's Arnaud Costes celebrates victory.

1999

France 43 New Zealand 31

New Zealand were massive favourites going into this semi-final, with France only showing glimpses of their best form in the pool stages and quarter-finals. The French were, however, very relaxed.

Initially, despite the sparkling form of Christophe Dominici who created a try for Christophe Lamaison, the All Blacks pulled ahead very much as expected and the game seemed to be over five minutes into the second half when Jonah Lomu waltzed in virtually unopposed for his second try. From that point onwards, however, it was all France as they scored 33 points straight off and raced to possibly their most famous ever victory.

Lamaison, who eventually garnered a match total of 28 points, started the comeback with two clever dropped goals, which finally gave France some momentum. Then came brilliant tries by Dominici, Richard Dourthe and Philippe Bernat-Salles as France piled on the agony and built a match-winning 43–24 lead. New Zealand salvaged a little pride with a late try by Jeff Wilson but they were well and truly beaten and the All Blacks knew it.

Probably only France could turn a match on its head like that. It was a sensational victory and the sight of France parading around Twickenham, being acclaimed by a largely English crowd was something to behold. In a symbolic gesture, shortly after the final whistle, Josh Kronfeld handed his scrum-cap to opposite number Olivier Magne, a vanquished warrior acknowledging a new hero.

Glossary of Terms

Added time
Time added on after injuries, delays and time spent consulting with the video ref.

Advantage
The referee can allow the game to proceed uninterrupted after an offence as long as he considers that the non-offending team has gained an advantage. If no advantage is gained the referee blows for the original offence.

Blind side
The side nearest to the touchline.

Blood-bin
Players are allowed a maximum of 15 minutes to go off the pitch to be treated for cuts.

Conversion
After a try is scored it is possible to score an extra two points by "converting" the try – that is, by kicking the ball between the posts from an imaginary line drawn out into the field of play from where the try was scored.

Drop-kick
A kick technique where the ball is dropped to the ground and kicked on the half-volley between the posts.

Dummy
A technique where a player pretends to pass the ball.

Extra time
Two periods, usually of 15 minutes each, when the game is drawn after full time.

Eye in the sky
See video referee.

Five-metre line
An interrupted line to indicate 5 metres from the try-line and 5 metres from the touchline.

Fourth official
A designated official who can take over as referee should the referee have to retire through injury.

Garryowen
A high ball aimed in the direction of the opposition full-back. A tactic that originated at the Garryowen club in Limerick, Ireland.

Half-time
Period, now universally of ten minutes, between each half.

Knock-on
Where a player drops the ball forward (towards the opponents' goal line).

Line-out
When two single-file lines are formed by forwards of the opposing teams after the ball goes out of touch.

Maul
A loose formation brought around a player who is still in possession of the ball and has not been brought to the ground. Some teams have perfected the art of "rolling" the maul forward, a tactic which often results in tries from short range.

Glossary of Terms

Obstruction
Also called blocking. Where a player gets in the way of an opponent who is chasing after the ball. This results in a penalty.

Off-side
Generally when a player is in front of the ball, not behind the last foot of the ruck or maul, or not back 10 yards on set plays.

Penalty kick
Kick awarded to the non-offending team after a penalty occurs. You can either place kick at goal in an attempt to score three points, tap the ball through the penalty mark and run the ball or kick directly to touch.

Place kick
A kicking technique where the ball is placed on the ground before being kicked between the posts for three points.

Left: **Australia's John Eales leaps high at a line-out.**

Punt
A kicking technique where the ball is dropped and kicked before it touches the ground.

Replacement
When an injured player is replaced by a fit player from the bench.

Ruck
A loose formation created around either a free ball or a player who has been brought to the ground with the ball.

Scrum (Scrummage)
When the two opposing sets of forwards (eight per team) pack down against each other.

Sin-bin
When a player is sent off the pitch for ten minutes, either because of foul play or for a "professional" foul which illegally prevents a probable score.

Sub
When the coach of a team decides to make a tactical switch, by taking one player off and putting another on.

The 22
A line marked out across the pitch exactly 22 metres from the try-line. It used to be the 25-yard line but changed when the game went metric. Within that area you are allowed to kick the ball directly into touch.

Try
Method of scoring worth 5 points by touching the ball down in the opponents' goal area.

Video referee
When there is a disputed try decision the referee can ask another official sitting next to TV monitors in the stadium to adjudicate.

Below: **England's Martin Johnson tries to ruck the ball clear.**

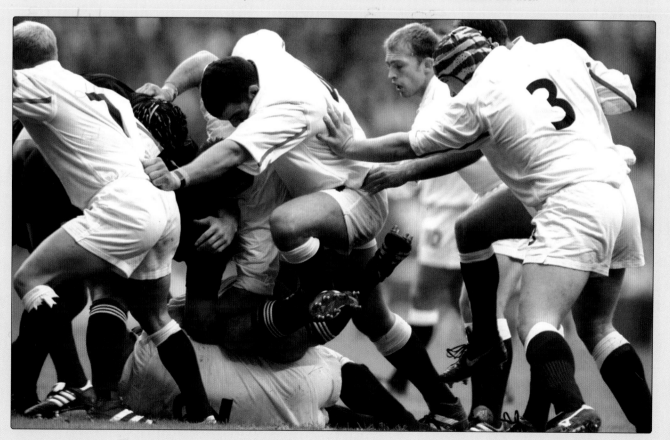

Guide to the RUGBY

POOL A

Australia **Argentina** **Ireland** **Namibia** **Romania**

Friday, October 10
Australia v Argentina · Sydney
Score: 24 — 8

Saturday, October 11
Ireland v Romania · Gosford
Score: 45 — 17

Tuesday, October 14
Argentina v Namibia · Gosford
Score: 67 — 14

Saturday, October 18
Australia v Romania · Brisbane
Score: 90 — 8

Sunday, October 19
Ireland v Namibia · Sydney
Score: 64 — 7

Wednesday, October 22
Argentina v Romnia · Sydney
Score: 50 — 3

Saturday, October 25
Australia v Namibia · Adelaide
Score: 142 — 0

Sunday, October 26
Argentina v Ireland · Adelaide
Score: 15 — 16

Thursday, October 30
Namibia v Romania · Launceston
Score: 7 — 37

Saturday, November 1
Australia v Ireland · Melbourne
Score: 17 — 16

POOL B

France **Scotland** **Fiji** **Japan** **USA**

Saturday, October 11
France v Fiji · Brisbane
Score: 61 — 18

Sunday, October 12
Scotland v Japan · Townsville
Score: 32 — 11

Wednesday, October 15
Fiji v USA · Brisbane
Score: 19 — 18

Saturday, October 18
France v Japan · Townsville
Score: 51 — 29

Monday, October 20
Scotland v USA · Brisbane
Score: 39 — 15

Thursday, October 23
Fiji v Japan · Townsville
Score: 41 — 13

Saturday, October 25
France v Scotland · Sydney
Score: 51 — 9

Monday, October 27
Japan v USA · Gosford
Score: 26 — 39

Friday, October 31
France v USA · Wollongong
Score: 41 — 14

Saturday, November 1
Scotland v Fiji · Sydney
Score: 22 — 20

Quarter-finals

Saturday, November 8
Winner Pool D v Runner-up Pool C
Melbourne
NZ29 SA9

Saturday, November 8
Winner Pool A v Runner-up Pool B
Brisbane
Aus 33 Sco 16

Sunday, November 9
Winner Pool B v Runner-up Pool A
Melbourne
Fra 43 Ire 21

Sunday, November 9
Winner Pool C v Runner-up Pool D
Brisbane
Eng 28 Wales 1

Semi-finals

Saturday, November 15
Winner QF1 v Winner QF2
Sydney
Aus 22 NZ 10

Sunday, November 16
Winner QF3 v Winner QF4
Sydney
Eng 24 Fra 7

WORLD CUP 2003

POOL C

South Africa **England** **Samoa** **Georgia** **Uruguay**

Saturday, October 11
South Africa v Uruguay · Perth
Score: 72 — 6

Sunday, October 12
England v Georgia · Perth
Score: 94 — 6

Wednesday, October 15
Samoa v Uruguay · Perth
Score: 60 — 13

Saturday, October 18
South Africa v England · Perth
Score: 6 — 25

Sunday, October 19
Georgia v Samoa · Perth
Score: 9 — 46

Friday, October 24
South Africa v Georgia · Sydney
Score: 46 — 19

Sunday, October 26
England v Samoa · Melbourne
Score: 35 — 22

Tuesday, October 28
Georgia v Uruguay · Sydney
Score: 12 — 24

Saturday, November 1
South Africa v Samoa · Brisbane
Score: 60 — 10

Sunday, November 2
England v Uruguay · Brisbane
Score: 111 — 13

POOL D

New Zealand **Wales** **Italy** **Canada** **Tonga**

Saturday, October 11
New Zealand v Italy · Melbourne
Score: 70 — 7

Sunday, October 12
Wales v Canada · Melbourne
Score: 41 — 10

Wednesday, October 15
Italy v Tonga · Canberra
Score: 36 — 12

Friday, October 17
New Zealand v Canada · Melbourne
Score: 68 — 6

Sunday, October 19
Wales v Tonga · Canberra
Score: 27 — 20

Tuesday, October 21
Italy v Canada · Canberra
Score: 19 — 14

Friday, October 24
New Zealand v Tonga · Brisbane
Score: 91 — 7

Saturday, October 25
Italy v Wales · Canberra
Score: 15 — 27

Wednesday, October 29
Canada v Tonga · Wollongong
Score: 24 — 7

Sunday, November 2
New Zealand v Wales · Sydney
Score: 53 — 37

Third-place Play-off

Thursday, November 20
Loser SF1 v **Loser SF2** · Sydney

NZ 40   Fra 13

Final

Saturday, November 22
Winner SF1 v **Winner SF2** · Sydney

Eng 20   Aus 17

Answers to questions on pages 66–67

Quiz answers

1　Australia

2　Wales (in 2002)

3　New Zealand

4　Colonial Stadium, Melbourne

5　Australia

6　Didier Camberabero

7　110–0

8　Webb Ellis Trophy

9　Third, 1987, Australia, Rotorua, NZ

10　Marc Ellis, 6 tries for
　　New Zealand v Japan 1987

11　David Kirk

12　Michael Jones, New Zealand

13　Serge Blanco

14　Croatia

15　(c) 1.7 million

16　(b) 98

17　Gavin Hastings, Scotland, 227 points

18　Keith Wood (Ireland v USA, 1999),
　　Brian Robinson (Ireland v Zimbabwe,
　　1991)

19　New Zealand 145 Japan 17

20　Gareth Rees

21　Ralph Keyes (Ireland)

22　South Africa 1995

23　Juan Grobler (USA v Australia)

24　Jonah Lomu with 15 tries

25　Joel Stransky

What's in a name?

A　Jonathan Davies

B　David Campese

C　Neil Back

D　Frano Botica

E　Philippe Sella

F　Andy Irvine

G　Gary Teichman

H　Michael Owen

I　Mark Ella

J　Dorian West

K　Serge Blanco

L　Michael Lynagh

M　Mefin Davies

N　John Tait

O　Tim Rodber

Picture Credits